everyday French

Quel temps fait-il ?

Alison Clarke &
Heather Crabtree

Credits and acknowledgements

Minimum specification

PC or Mac with CD-ROM drive and 512 Mb RAM (recommended)

Windows 2000 or above/Mac OSX 10.4

Recommended minimum processor speed: 1.3 Ghz

Acknowledgements

The publishers gratefully acknowledge permission to reproduce the following copyright material:

Cartes Cochons for the use of '*Quel temps fait-il aujourd 'hui ?*' from *Allez Hop ! Chantez !* by Alison Middleton and Anne Oliver © 2008, Alison Middleton © (2008, Cartes Cochons).

© Crown copyright material. Reproduced under the terms of the Click Use licence.

Every effort has been made to trace copyright holders for the works reproduced in this book, and the publishers apologise for any inadvertent omissions.

Due to the nature of the web, we cannot guarantee the content or links of any website mentioned. We strongly recommend that teachers check websites before using them in the classroom.

Authors
Alison Clarke &
Heather Crabtree

Commissioning Editor
Juliet Gladston

Development Editors
Niamh O'Carroll,
Kate Pedlar & Fabia Lewis

Project Editor
Gina Thorsby

Editor
Alex Albrighton

Series Designers and Cover Artwork
Sonja Bagley &
Joy Monkhouse

Illustrations
Moreno Chiacchiera &
Jackie Stafford/Beehive Illustration

Designer
Sonja Bagley

CD-ROM design and development team
Joy Monkhouse,
Allison Parry, Andrea Lewis,
Anna Oliwa, Shelley Best &
Haremi

Cover images
Umbrella © stockxpert.com
Sunset ©Galyna Andrushko /www.shutterstock.com

Designed using Adobe Indesign
Published by Scholastic Ltd
Book End, Range Road,
Witney,
Oxfordshire, OX29 OYD
www.scholastic.co.uk

Printed by Bell & Bain Ltd, Glasgow

1 2 3 4 5 6 7 8 9   0 1 2 3 4 5 6 7 8 9

British Library Cataloguing-in-Publication Data
A catalogue record for this book is available from the British Library.
ISBN 978-1407-10206-1

Contents

Resources on the CD-ROM

Unit 1

Interactive flashcard: *Par tous les temps 1*
Interactive flashcard: *Par tous les temps 2*
Interactive activity: *Par tous les temps*
Photocopiable: *Par tous les temps*
Images: *La pluie, Le soleil, La neige, Le vent, L'orage*

Unit 2

Interactive flashcard: *Quand il fait beau ...*
Interactive activity: *Quand il fait beau ...*
Photocopiable: *Quand il fait beau ...*

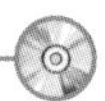

Unit 3

Interactive flashcard: *Quel temps fait-il à Blois ?*
Interactive activity: *Quel temps fait-il à Blois ?*
Photocopiable: *Quel temps fait-il en Suisse ?*

Unit 4

Interactive flashcard: *Les mois 1*
Interactive flashcard: *Les mois 2*
Interactive flashcard: *Les saisons*
Interactive activity: *C'est en quelle saison ?*
Photocopiable: *Mon calendrier*

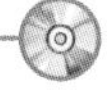

Unit 5

Interactive flashcard: *Mets ton chapeau ! 1*
Interactive flashcard: *Mets ton chapeau ! 2*
Interactive activity: *Qu'est-ce que je mets ?*
Photocopiable: *Mes vêtements*
Film: *Mets ton chapeau !*
Film transcript: *Mets ton chapeau !*

Unit 6

Interactive flashcard: *Bienvenue au Sénégal !*
Interactive activity: *C'est où ?*
Photocopiable: *Le baobab d'Afrique*
Translation: *Le baobab d'Afrique*

Unit 7

Interactive flashcard: *L'hiver au Québec*
Interactive activity: *Au Québec*
Photocopiable: *Les animaux de la forêt québécoise*
Translation: *Les animaux de la forêt québécoise*

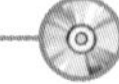

Unit 8

Interactive flashcard: *Le cycle de l'eau*
Interactive activity: *Le cycle de l'eau*
Photocopiable: *Le cycle de l'eau*
Translation: *Le cycle de l'eau*

Unit 9

Interactive flashcard: *On parle français en Europe*
Interactive activity: *On parle français en Europe*
Photocopiable: *Quel temps fait-il en Europe ?*

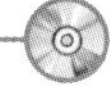

Unit 10

Interactive flashcard: *Quel temps fait-il aujourd'hui ?*
Interactive activity: *Quel temps fait-il aujourd'hui ?*
Photocopiable: *Les dominos*
Photocopiable: *Quel temps fait-il aujourd'hui ?*
Song: *Quel temps fait-il aujourd'hui ?*
Translation: *Quel temps fait-il aujourd'hui ?*

Unit 11

Interactive flashcard: *Eric l'épouvantail*
Interactive activity: *Eric l'épouvantail*
Photocopiable: *Ecris et dessine*

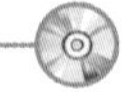

Unit 12

Interactive flashcard: *En colonie de vacances*
Interactive activity: *Une carte postale*
Photocopiable: *Jeux*
Photocopiable: *Où vas-tu passer les vacances ?*
Song: *Où vas-tu passer les vacances ?*
Translation: *Où vas-tu passer les vacances ?*

Introduction

Introduction

The activities in this book are intended to be practical and enjoyable while at the same time laying some sound foundations for language learning. Most of the units can be taught independently of the others, while others build on previous units.

On pages 8–9 there is a grid linking the units to the KS2 Framework for Languages indicating the relevant strand and, where appropriate, objective, and using the usual abbreviations:

O = Oracy
L = Literacy
IU = Intercultural understanding
LLS = Language learning strategies
KAL = Knowledge about language

Introducing new core vocabulary

- Always make sure the children are watching and listening. Get into a routine of saying ***Regardez !*** (Watch!) – make a spectacles shape with your fingers or point to your eyes; ***Écoutez !*** (Listen!) – gesture to your ears;
- Choose the simplest phrases to introduce first – especially if they are 'cognates' (look or sound like their English equivalents). This builds confidence!
- Only teach a few phrases at a time – so, to start with, try, for example, ***il pleut***, ***il neige*** and ***il fait chaud***. Play a couple of simple games (see below) then introduce the others.
- Point to/hold up the flashcard as you say the phrase.
- Use gestures to reinforce the meaning, for example, a downward movement of the hand with 'fluttery' fingers for ***il neige*** (it's snowing).

Games for practising vocabulary

- **Répétez si c'est vrai** – Hold up a flashcard or object and say a word or phrase. The children repeat only if what the teacher says matches the picture or object she is holding.
- **Secret signal** – Sit the children in a horseshoe shape so that they can see each other. Display all the vocabulary items learned in a clear 'list' form. Choose one child to be the 'detective' who will go outside the room (accompanied by a TA perhaps). Choose another child to be the 'secret signaller'. Explain to the children that you are all going to chant the words/phrases, starting with the one at the beginning of the list. When the secret signaller makes the secret signal (for example, rubbing the forehead or scratching an ear) you will all start chanting the next phrase in the list. The aim of the game is for the secret signaller to avoid detection and for the class to chant the phrases for as long as possible.

Introduction

- **Quick whizz** – Put picture cards in a pile with their pictures hidden from the class. Make a play of 'shuffling' the cards. Ask the children to say the word or phrase together when they can see what it is. Take the top one and quickly 'whizz' it, picture facing the children, but making it disappear again very quickly. Repeat as many times as you wish. Keep shuffling and emphasising that it's a game. From the teacher's point of view, this game is about getting the children to practise words and phrases; for the children it's about being the fastest and most observant.
- **Fly swat** – You need two plastic fly-swats and a set of flashcards fixed to a wall or board with sticky putty. The class is divided into two teams and children take turns to come forward. The teacher calls out a phrase/word. The first person to swat the correct flashcard wins a point for his/her team.
- **Salade de fruits** – The purpose of this game is to get children listening (and responding) to language. The children sit on the floor in a circle. Choose a limited number of vocabulary items. Give each child a word/phrase to remember, so that several children have the same phrase. When the teacher calls out one of the words or phrases the children with that phrase must stand up and change places. Now and then, call out ***salade de fruits*** and all must change places.
- **Hot/cold** – This game is excellent for whole-class practice of a 'hard to pronounce' word or phrase, such as ***Quel temps fait-il aujourd'hui ?*** (What is the weather like today?). The seeker is sent out of the room, while the teacher or child hides the object or flashcard. As the seeker re-enters the room, the class begins to chant the word or phrase repeatedly and rhythmically, getting louder as they get closer, or softer as they move further away, until the object is found.
- **Morpion** (noughts and crosses) – On your class whiteboard, or using an interactive whiteboard, draw a 3 x 3 grid. Stick a word card in each of the squares so that the children can identify their chosen square. Divide the class into two teams – ***les cercles*** (o) ***et les croix*** (x). Tell the class: ***choisissez une case*** (choose a square). Teams take turns to choose a square and a member of the team must say the word on that flashcard to place their nought or cross on the board.

Introducing the written word

- Make reading cards for new words and phrases, so that you can introduce the written form of the new language you have taught in a planned and systematic way.
- When you show the children new word cards, always get them to read them aloud with you, insisting on correct pronunciation.
- Ask the children to tell you about 'surprises' in the spellings (eg silent ***s*** or ***t*** at the ends of words).
- Encourage the children to look out for rhymes and patterns, pointing out which vowels make which sounds in French (eg the letter ***i*** in ***petit***, ***il***, ***avril*** making a sound like the English 'ee').

The gender of nouns

- You may find it helpful to add a system of colour-coding to the word and picture cards (say, red for feminine, blue for masculine) to help children remember which words are masculine and which words are feminine.
- Always introduce nouns with a definite/indefinite article (eg ***le pantalon***, ***un pull***) never the noun on its own. This will help children to remember the gender of the noun.

How to use the CD-ROM

Here are brief guidance notes for using the CD-ROM. For more detailed information, see **How to use** on the start-up screen, or **Help** on the relevant screen for information about a particular resource.

The CD-ROM follows the structure of the book and contains:

- 12 on-screen interactive activities
- 12 on-screen interactive flashcards
- Audio songs
- Film clips
- Images and poster pages
- All of the photocopiable pages including the song lyrics and English translations

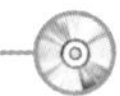

Getting started

To begin using the CD-ROM, simply place it in your CD- or DVD-ROM drive. Although the CD-ROM should auto run, if it fails to do so, navigate to the drive and double click on the red **Start** icon.

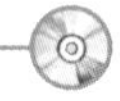

Start-up screen

The start-up screen is the first screen that appears. Here you can access: how to use the CD-ROM, terms and conditions, credits and registration links. If you agree to the terms and conditions, click **Start** to continue.

Main menu

The main menu provides links to all of the Units. Clicking on the relevant Unit icon will take you to the Unit screen where you can access all the Unit's resources. Clicking on **Resource finder** will take you to a search screen for all the resources, where you can search by key word or Unit for a specific resource.

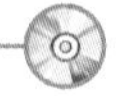

Resource finder

The **Resource finder** lists all of the resources on the CD-ROM. You can:

- Select a Unit by choosing the appropriate title from the drop-down menu.
- Search for key words by typing them into the search box.
- Scroll up or down the list of resources to locate the required resource.
- Launch a resource by clicking once on its row on the screen.

- Access the glossary of French words and English translations. (See more information below.)

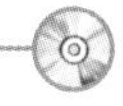

Navigation

The resources all open in separate windows on top of the menu screen. To close a resource, click on the arrow in the top right-hand corner of the screen. To return to the menu screen you can either close or minimise a resource.

Closing a resource will not close the program. However, if you are in a menu screen, then clicking on the **x** in the top right-hand corner of the screen will close the program. To return to a previous menu screen, you need to click on the **Back** arrow button.

Glossary

All of the interactive activities and interactive flashcards link to a glossary. The glossary will open in a separate window. Simply click first on the desired headletter and then on the French word to reveal the English translation. You can also click on the audio buttons to hear the pronunciation of each French word.

Whiteboard tools

The CD-ROM comes with its own set of whiteboard tools for use on any whiteboard. These include:

- Pen tool
- Highlighter tool
- Eraser
- Sticky note

Click on the **Tools** button on the right-hand side of the screen to access these tools.

Printing

Print the resources by clicking on the **Print** button. The photocopiable pages print as full A4 portrait pages, but please note if you have a landscape photocopiable page or poster you need to set the orientation to landscape in your print preferences. Printouts of the interactive activities will include what is on the screen. For a full A4 printout you need to set the orientation to landscape in your print preferences.

Framework links

Unit	Oracy	Literacy	Knowledge about language	IU	Language and learning strategies
1	3.2, 3.4 4.2, 4.4 5.1 6.4	3.1, 3.2, 3.3 4.1, 4.3 5.2 6.4	**Year 3:** Identify specific sounds, phonemes and words; imitate pronunciation of sounds; recognise question forms; notice the spelling of familiar words. **Year 4:** Reinforce and extend recognition of word classes and understand their function; use question forms. **Year 5:** Recognise patterns in simple sentences; manipulate language by changing an element in a sentence; develop accuracy in pronunciation and intonation. **Year 6:** Use knowledge of words, text and structure to build simple spoken and written passages; devise questions for authentic use.		• Use actions and rhymes and play games to aid memorisation. • Look at the face of the person speaking and listen attentively. • Use gestures to show they understand. • Read and memorise words.
2	3.2, 3.3 4.2, 4.4 5.1, 5.2 6.4	3.1, 3.2, 3.3 4.1, 4.3, 4.4 5.2 6.4	**Year 3:** Identify specific sounds, phonemes and words; imitate pronunciation of sounds; recognise question forms and negatives; notice the spelling of familiar words. **Year 4:** Reinforce and extend recognition of word classes and understand their function; use question forms. **Year 5:** Recognise patterns in simple sentences; manipulate language by changing an element in a sentence; develop accuracy in pronunciation and intonation; understand and use negatives; recognise the typical conventions of word order in the foreign language. **Year 6:** Recognise patterns in the foreign language; use knowledge of words, text and structure to build simple spoken and written passages; devise questions for authentic use.		• Use actions and rhymes and play games to aid memorisation. • Look at the face of the person speaking and listen attentively. • Use gestures to show they understand. • Write new words. • Compare the language with English. • Read and memorise words.
3	3.1, 3.2, 3.3 4.1, 4.2, 4.3, 4.4 5.1 6.1, 6.4	3.1, 3.2, 3.3 4.1, 4.3, 4.4 5.2, 5.3 6.1, 6.4	**Year 3:** Identify specific sounds, phonemes and words; recognise commonly used rhyming sounds; imitate pronunciation of sounds; recognise question forms; recognise how sounds are represented in written form; notice the spelling of familiar words. **Year 4:** Reinforce and extend recognition of word classes and understand their function; recognise and apply simple agreements; use question forms. **Year 5:** Recognise patterns in simple sentences; manipulate language by changing an element in a sentence; apply knowledge of rules when building sentences; develop accuracy in pronunciation and intonation. **Year 6:** Recognise patterns in the foreign language; notice and match agreements; use knowledge of words, text and structure to build simple spoken and written passages; devise questions for authentic use.	3.2	• Use actions and rhymes and play games to aid memorisation. • Look at the face of the person speaking and listen attentively. • Remember rhyming words. • Practise new language with a friend. • Write new words. • Read and memorise words.
4	3.2, 3.3, 3.4 4.2, 4.3, 4.4 5.1 6.4	3.1, 3.2 4.1, 4.3 5.2 6.3	**Year 3:** Identify specific sounds, phonemes and words; imitate pronunciation of sounds; recognise question forms; recognise how sounds are represented in written form; notice the spelling of familiar words. **Year 4:** Reinforce and extend recognition of word classes and understand their function; recognise and apply simple agreements; use question forms; identify a different writing system. **Year 5:** Recognise patterns in simple sentences; manipulate language by changing an element in a sentence; apply knowledge of rules when building sentences; develop accuracy in pronunciation and intonation; appreciate that different languages use different writing conventions. **Year 6:** Recognise patterns in the foreign language; notice and match agreements; use knowledge of words, text and structure to build simple spoken and written passages; devise questions for authentic use.	3.2 4.1 5.1	• Use actions and rhymes and play games to aid memorisation. • Look at the face of the person speaking and listen attentively. • Compare the language with English. • Use context and previous knowledge to determine meaning and pronunciation. • Read and memorise words. • Sort words into categories. • Look and listen for visual and aural clues.
5	3.2, 3.3 4.2, 4.4 5.1 6.4	3.1, 3.2 4.1, 4.2, 4.3 5.1 6.1	**Year 3:** Identify specific sounds, phonemes and words; imitate pronunciation of sounds; recognise question forms; recognise how sounds are represented in written form; notice the spelling of familiar words. **Year 4:** Reinforce and extend recognition of word classes and understand their function; recognise and apply simple agreements; use question forms. **Year 5:** Recognise patterns in simple sentences; manipulate language by changing an element in a sentence; apply knowledge of rules when building sentences; develop accuracy in pronunciation and intonation. **Year 6:** Recognise patterns in the foreign language; notice and match agreements; use knowledge of words, text and structure to build simple spoken and written passages; devise questions for authentic use.		• Use actions and rhymes and play games to aid memorisation. • Look at the face of the person speaking and listen attentively. • Compare the language with English. • Use context and previous knowledge to determine meaning and pronunciation. • Read and memorise words. • Look and listen for visual and aural clues.
6	3.2, 3.3 4.2 5.3 6.1, 6.3	3.1, 3.2 4.1, 4.2, 4.3 5.1 6.1	**Year 3:** Identify specific sounds, phonemes and words; imitate pronunciation of sounds; recognise negatives; recognise how sounds are represented in written form; notice the spelling of familiar words; recognise that many languages are spoken in the UK and across the world. **Year 4:** Reinforce and extend recognition of word classes and understand their function; apply phonic knowledge of the language to support reading. **Year 5:** Recognise patterns in simple sentences; understand negatives. **Year 6:** Recognise patterns in the foreign language; notice and match agreements; use knowledge of word order and sentence construction to support the understanding of the written text.	3.2, 4.2 5.1, 5.2	• Discuss language learning and share ideas and experience. • Use context and previous knowledge to determine meaning and pronunciation. • Practise new language with a friend. • Look and listen for visual and aural clues. • Access information sources. • Pronounce unknown words.

Framework links

Unit	Oracy	Literacy	Knowledge about language	IU	Language and learning strategies
7	3.2, 3.3 4.2 5.1, 5.3 6.1, 6.3	3.1, 3.2 4.1, 4.2, 4.3 5.1, 5.2 6.1, 6.3	**Year 3:** Identify specific sounds, phonemes and words; imitate pronunciation of sounds; recognise how sounds are represented in written form; notice the spelling of familiar words; recognise that many languages are spoken in the UK and across the world. **Year 4:** Reinforce and extend recognition of word classes and understand their function; apply phonic knowledge of the language to support reading. **Year 5:** Recognise patterns in simple sentences; manipulate language by changing an element in a sentence; apply knowledge of rules when building sentences; develop accuracy in pronunciation and intonation; recognise the typical conventions of word order in the foreign language. **Year 6:** Recognise patterns in the foreign language; use knowledge of word order and sentence construction to support the understanding of the written text.	3.3, 3.4 4.2 5.1, 5.2	• Discuss language learning and share ideas and experience. • Compare the language with English. • Use context and previous knowledge to determine meaning and pronunciation. • Read and memorise words. • Practise new language with a friend. • Look and listen for visual and aural clues. • Use a dictionary. • Access information sources. • Pronounce unknown words.
8	3.2, 3.3 4.2 5.3 6.1, 6.3	3.1, 3.2 4.1, 4.2, 4.3 5.1, 5.2 6.1, 6.3	**Year 3:** Identify specific sounds, phonemes and words; imitate pronunciation of sounds; recognise how sounds are represented in written form; notice the spelling of familiar words. **Year 4:** Reinforce and extend recognition of word classes and understand their function; apply phonic knowledge of the language to support reading; recognise that texts in different languages will often have the same conventions of style and layout. **Year 5:** Recognise patterns in simple sentences; apply knowledge of rules when building sentences; develop accuracy in pronunciation and intonation; recognise the typical conventions of word order in the foreign language. **Year 6:** Recognise patterns in the foreign language; use knowledge of word order and sentence construction to support the understanding of the written text.		• Discuss language learning and share ideas and experience. • Play games to aid memorisation. • Compare the language with English. • Use context and previous knowledge to determine meaning and pronunciation. • Read and memorise words. • Look and listen for visual and aural clues. • Use a dictionary. • Pronounce unknown words.
9	3.2, 3.3 4.2, 4.4 5.3 6.1, 6.3	3.1, 3.2, 3.3 4.1, 4.2 5.1 6.1	**Year 3:** Identify specific sounds, phonemes and words; imitate pronunciation of sounds; hear main word classes, recognise question forms; recognise how sounds are represented in written form; notice the spelling of familiar words. **Year 4:** Reinforce and extend recognition of word classes and understand their function; recognise and apply simple agreements; use question forms; apply phonic knowledge of the language to support reading. **Year 5:** Recognise patterns in simple sentences; apply knowledge of rules when building sentences; develop accuracy in pronunciation and intonation; recognise the typical conventions of word order in the foreign language. **Year 6:** Recognise patterns in the foreign language; notice and match agreements; use knowledge of word order and sentence construction to support the understanding of the written text; devise questions for authentic use.	3.2, 3.4 4.2, 5.2	• Discuss language learning and share ideas and experience. • Play games to aid memorisation . • Use context and previous knowledge to determine meaning and pronunciation. • Use language known in one context in another context. • Read and memorise words. • Look and listen for visual and aural clues.
10	3.1, 3.2, 3.3 4.1, 4.2, 4.3, 4.4 5.1, 5.4 6.1, 6.2	3.1, 3.2 4.1, 4.2, 4.3 5.1 6.1	**Year 3:** Identify specific sounds, phonemes and words; recognise commonly used rhyming sounds; imitate pronunciation of sounds; recognise question forms; recognise how sounds are represented in written form; notice the spelling of familiar words. **Year 4:** Reinforce and extend recognition of word classes and understand their function; use question forms; apply phonic knowledge of the language to support reading. **Year 5:** Recognise patterns in simple sentences; develop accuracy in pronunciation and intonation; recognise the typical conventions of word order in the foreign language. **Year 6:** Recognise patterns in the foreign language; use knowledge of word order and sentence construction to support the understanding of the written text.		• Use actions and rhymes and play games to aid memorisation. • Remember rhyming words. • Practise new language with a friend. • Read and memorise words. • Look and listen for visual and aural clues.
11	3.2, 3.3 4.2 5.2, 5.3, 5.4 6.1, 6.2	3.1, 3.2, 3.3 4.1, 4.2, 4.3, 4.4 5.1, 5.3 6.1, 6.4	**Year 3:** Identify specific sounds, phonemes and words; imitate pronunciation of sounds; recognise how sounds are represented in written form; notice the spelling of familiar words. **Year 4:** Reinforce and extend recognition of word classes and understand their function; recognise and apply simple agreements, singular and plural. **Year 5:** Recognise patterns in simple sentences; manipulate language by changing an element in a sentence; apply knowledge of rules when building sentences; develop accuracy in pronunciation and intonation. **Year 6:** Recognise patterns in the foreign language; notice and match agreements; use knowledge of words, text and structure to build simple spoken and written passages.		• Use actions and rhymes and play games to aid memorisation. • Compare the language with English. • Use context and previous knowledge to determine meaning and pronunciation. • Read and memorise words. • Look and listen for visual and aural clues.
12	3.2, 3.3 4.2 5.2, 5.3 6.3	3.1, 3.2, 3.3 4.1,4.2, 4.3, 4.4 5.1, 5.2, 5.3 6.1, 6.3, 6.4	**Year 3:** Identify specific sounds, phonemes and words; imitate pronunciation of sounds; recognise negatives; recognise how sounds are represented in written form; notice the spelling of familiar words. **Year 4:** Reinforce and extend recognition of word classes and understand their function; apply phonic knowledge of the language to support reading and writing. **Year 5:** Recognise patterns in simple sentences; manipulate language by changing an element in a sentence; apply knowledge of rules when building sentences; develop accuracy in pronunciation and intonation; understand and use negatives; recognise the typical conventions of word order in the foreign language. **Year 6:** Recognise patterns in the foreign language; use knowledge of words, text and structure to build simple spoken and written passages; use knowledge of word order and sentence construction to support the understanding of the written text.	3.2, 3.3, 3.4 4.2 5.1 6.1, 6.2	• Use actions and rhymes and play games to aid memorisation. • Practise new language with a friend. • Use context and previous knowledge to determine meaning and pronunciation. • Read and memorise words. • Access information sources. • Look and listen for visual and aural clues.

Unit 1: Par tous les temps

Objectives

To understand and be able to say a range of weather phrases and to ask what the weather is like; to be able to read and copy-write key weather phrases.

Introducing the vocabulary

- Using 'Interactive flashcard: ***Par tous les temps 1***' click on the title to introduce ***Quel temps fait-il ?*** Now click on the sky area of picture 1 and the clouds in picture 2 to introduce ***il fait beau*** and ***il fait mauvais***. Encourage the children to listen to the audio a few times before you ask them to repeat. Praise accuracy of pronunciation.
- Repeat this exercise for the other weather phrases on the flashcard – ***il fait du soleil***, ***il fait chaud and il pleut***. Use 'Interactive flashcard: '***Par tous les temps 2***' to introduce the weather phrases ***il neige***, ***il fait froid*** and ***il fait du vent***.
- Make a commonly agreed gesture for each weather phrase, for example, your hand descending with 'fluttery' fingers for ***il neige***.
- Make your own reading cards of the vocabulary in this unit. Ask the children to look out for patterns and surprises when they see the phrases written down for the first time, such as silent letters at the ends of words.
- Continue to practise the weather phrases using the photographs on the CD-ROM and some of the games suggested in the Introduction (see pages 5–6) such as 'Secret signal', ***Salade de fruits*** and 'Hot/cold'.

Vocabulary extension

- For children who are comfortable with the weather phrases on the interactive flashcards introduce ***il fait du brouillard*** and ***il fait de l'orage***. Ask them to think up actions that might accompany these phrases and then draw their own flashcards.

Resources

Interactive flashcards:
Par tous les temps 1
Par tous les temps 2

Interactive activity:
Par tous les temps

Photocopiable page 34:
Par tous les temps

Images: ***La pluie, Le soleil, La neige, Le vent, L'orage***

Preparation

Make a set of cards for each pair or small group of children using Photocopiable 34: ***Par tous les temps***

Interactive whiteboard

Core activities

- Practise the question ***Quel temps fait-il ?*** with the whole class. If some of the children are finding the pronunciation hard, try a game of Hot/cold to get them practising (see Introduction).
- When the children are comfortable using the weather phrases, play a game using the sets of playing cards you have made from photocopiable page 34 (***Par tous les temps***). Ask the children to play in pairs or groups of three or four, perhaps with a teaching assistant or helper if available.
- To begin, one child shuffles the cards (***battre les cartes***), then turns the pile face down. Player one asks ***Quel temps fait-il ?*** Player two turns over the top card and answers according to their card. They then ask the next child or their partner ***Quel temps fait-il ?***
- You can use two sets of cards for each group to play ***Le jeu de paires*** (Pelmanism). Shuffle the cards and spread them out face down. Players take turns to turn over two cards, saying the weather phrases as they do so. If they turn over a matching pair, the child may keep those cards. The winner is the child with the greatest number of pairs.
- Use 'Interactive activity: ***Par tous les temps***' to consolidate this learning. Children have to match the French phrases to the correct picture or English translation.

Extension activities

- Play a variation on ***Le jeu de paires***. Substitute a matching set of weather reading cards for one set of picture cards. Children must again say/read what is on their cards as they turn them over.
- As the children become more confident, use your picture and reading cards to make a weather chart. Build in differentiation by asking one child to choose the correct picture card, another to say the phrase, another to ask the question and another to find the correct reading card. Ask for more than one weather phrase for each day.

Tips

Make a set of A5 or A4 weather picture flashcards to use to support the activities – or ask the children to make them for you (see ICT activity, right).

Cross-curricular ideas

Art and design: To design and make a mobile.
Children can design and make a simple collaged weather mobile for classroom display that includes pictures and text. Encourage them to choose appropriate materials to produce desired textures and weather effects.

Literacy: To write a simple instruction text.
When the children are familiar with the rules for ***Le jeu de paires*** encourage them to write out their own version as if they were explaining the game to a child in another class.

ICT: To create picture flashcards using text and images.
Encourage the children to make simple weather cards for display by typing out a phrase and illustrating it using Clip Art or their own pictures either scanned in or created using drawing software.

Five-minute follow-ups

- Continue to play games as described above to reinforce vocabulary.
- Check out the weather in France by looking at a French weather website such as **http://france.meteofrance.com/** or invite the children to find and translate the weather for your area using a website such as **www.bbc.co.uk/weather**
- Hand out weather picture cards to pairs of children. Ask the children to make a logical weather sentence using as many components as possible, linking them together with appropriate conjunctions (***et/mais***). Sentences must not be contradictory, for example, ***il fait mauvais et il fait du soleil*** would not work.
- Select a child to mime a weather phrase. Then ask the other children in the class to guess the phrase and say it in French.

Key words

Core:

le temps – the weather
beau – fine
chaud – warm/hot
froid – cold
la pluie – the rain
la neige – the snow
le vent – the wind
mauvais – bad
le soleil – the sun
le jeu de paires – Pelmanism

Key phrases

Quel temps fait-il ? – What is the weather like?
il fait beau – the weather is fine
il fait mauvais – the weather is bad
il fait du soleil – it's sunny
il fait chaud – it's warm/hot
il fait froid – it's cold
il pleut – it's raining
il neige – it's snowing
il fait du vent – it's windy
en automne – in autumn
en hiver – in winter
en été – in summer
au printemps – in spring

Extension:

il fait du brouillard – it's foggy
il fait de l'orage – it's stormy
battre les cartes – to shuffle the cards

Language points

- Most weather phrases are made with ***il fait*** ....***Il fait*** comes from the verb ***faire***, which in English we often translate as 'to make' or 'to do'. Avoid translating it when talking about the weather.
- ***Faire*** is used for a huge range of other meanings as well. Many of them are used to talk about sports and hobbies (but strangely, not many can be translated as 'make' or 'do').

Unit 2: Quand il fait beau ...

Objectives

To discuss activities children like doing when the weather is good or bad; to write about favourite activities.

Introducing the vocabulary

- Show the children 'Interactive flashcard: ***Quand il fait beau ...***' and click on the girl and then the boy. Ask the children what sort of weather is mentioned by the girl and boy (***il fait beau*** and ***il fait mauvais***). Encourage the children to think of a mime or gesture for each activity shown – for example, cycling legs for ***faire du vélo***.
- Click on each of the hot spots and listen to the audio while the children mime the activities.
- Call out activities at random – for example, ***j'aime jouer au foot*** – and ask the children to do the appropriate mime.
- Encourage the children to repeat the audio for themselves as they click on the hot spots on the flashcard.

Core activities

- Using mime or gesture, play ***Jacques a dit*** (the French equivalent of 'Simon says') to make sure children have understood the activity vocabulary.
- Introduce ***j'aime*** to the class. Take a giant dice and stick pictures of the activities they have learned on the faces of the dice using masking tape or Blu-Tack®.
- Model how to throw the dice and say, for example, ***j'aime aller à la plage***, according to the top face of the dice. Do this with a smiley face or place a hand on your heart. Check that the children have understood.
- Now invite the children to stand in a circle and take turns to throw the dice and respond. Add a second dice for more challenge. Children must throw both and tell you two things they like doing using ***et*** (and) to join the phrases.
- Use 'Interactive activity: ***Quand il fait beau ...***' to let children decide for themselves what they like doing in fine and bad weather. The children should double click on each sentence to hear them before they choose what they like to do. Tell them that they do not need to place all the sentences. The activity is unmarked, but make sure that children can explain in English why they like to do each activity in the weather they choose. Print off the children's work and compare their responses.
- Give the children a sheet with pictures of the activities they have learned. Tell them they must find one person who likes doing each of those activities and write their name next to each picture. The children should ask each other: ***Tu aimes aller à la plage ? Tu aimes jouer au foot ?*** Feed back the results as a whole class and find out which is their favourite activity.
- Give each child a copy of photocopiable page 35 (***Quand il fait beau ...***) and ask them to draw and write about activities that they enjoy in fine and bad weather. Display the vocabulary to help them.

Extension activities

- Teach the children ***je n'aime pas*** (I don't like). Play the two-dice game as above, but stick three smiley and three sad faces to the faces of one of the dice.
- Add further challenge by introducing ***jouer au tennis***, ***jouer au rugby*** and ***jouer au basket***. These are cognates – that is, they look and sound like their English equivalents.

Resources

Interactive flashcard: ***Quand il fait beau ...***

Interactive activity: ***Quand il fait beau ...***

Photocopiable page 35: ***Quand il fait beau ...***

Preparation

Two giant dice

Masking tape or Blu-Tack®

You will also need a set of simple picture cards that are the same size as the sides of the dice showing the beach, cycling, football, skipping, cinema, friends, a dog, swimming pool, tennis, rugby, computer (use Clip Art or draw your own)

Interactive whiteboard

Tips

As the children learn the vocabulary for more activities and sports, create more picture cards and practise the new words using the dice game described on page 12.

Cross-curricular ideas

Maths: To collect and record data.

Use the data that the children gather about their favourite activities to build a pie chart or bar chart. Children can also ask another class about their preferences and compare the results.

PE: To use mimes of different sports as warm-up and cool-down exercises.

Demonstrate energetic, but on-the-spot, mimes for ***jouer au foot***, ***aller à la piscine***, ***sauter à la corde***, ***faire du vélo*** and so on. Call out these activities in French and encourage the children to do the mimes before they begin their PE lesson. The less energetic activities such as ***jouer avec mon chien*** or ***aller à la plage*** could be built into a similar cool-down activity.

Five-minute follow-ups

- Play ***Morpion*** (Noughts and crosses) to practise the new activity phrases (see Introduction, pages 5–6).
- Make a chain with the whole class or a group of children sitting or standing in a circle. Start the activity by asking ***Tu aimes sauter à la corde ?*** The child next to you must answer ***Oui, j'aime sauter à la corde*** or ***Non*** with an alternative activity that they enjoy. They can use the negative if they are confident. The answering child must then turn to the next and ask ***Tu aimes … ?*** and so on. Aim to get around the whole circle.
- Make some big reading cards of the words and phrases for this unit – for example, ***j'aime***; ***quand***; ***il fait beau***; ***il fait mauvais***; ***aller à la piscine***; ***jouer au foot***. Distribute the cards and encourage the children to build up a 'human sentence'. Include punctuation cards, too.

Key words

Core:

quand – when
j'aime – I like
jouer – to play/playing
jouer au foot(ball) – to play/playing football
avec – with
mes copains (m) – my friends
mon chien – my dog
aller – to go/going
aller au cinéma – to go/going to the cinema
aller à la plage – to go/going to the beach
sauter à la corde – to skip/skipping
faire du vélo – to cycle/cycling

Extension:

jouer à l'ordinateur – to play/playing on the computer
jouer au tennis – to play/playing tennis
jouer au rugby – to play/playing rugby
jouer au basket – to play/playing basketball
danser – to dance/dancing

Key phrases

Core:

quand il fait beau … – when the weather is fine...
quand il fait mauvais … – when the weather is bad...
Tu aimes … ? – Do you like...?
j'aime … + infinitive – I like...

Extension:

je n'aime pas … + infinitive – I don't like...
aller à la piscine – to go/going to the swimming pool

Language points

- ***Quand*** means 'when' and can be used to ask and to answer a question.
- To say what you like doing, use ***j'aime*** plus the infinitive (the part of the verb that means to do something). For example, ***j'aime jouer au foot*** (I like to play football); ***j'aime danser*** (I like to dance).
- The rule for making a negative is that you put ***ne*** and ***pas*** around the verb. Here, to say 'I don't like...' you must use ***n'*** rather than ***ne***, because ***aime*** begins with a vowel.

Unit 3: Nord, sud, est, ouest

Objectives

To understand and say the points of the compass in French; to listen and respond to a simple rhyme; to know the locations of some French and Belgian towns.

Resources

Interactive flashcard: ***Quel temps fait-il à Blois ?***

Interactive activity: ***Quel temps fait-il à Blois ?***

Photocopiable page 36: ***Quel temps fait-il en Suisse ?***

Preparation

Large compass or picture of a compass

Large map of France (optional)

Whiteboards and pens

You may like to make a set of flashcards with names of cities in France and Belgium written on. These could include the whole sentence: ***Quel temps fait-il à Paris ?***

Interactive whiteboard

Introducing the vocabulary

- Display 'Interactive flashcard: ***Quel temps fait-il à Blois ?***' As a class, look at each place and decide what the weather phrase is, then click on it and listen. Ask the children what they notice about the sound of the name of the place and the weather.
- When you have clicked on each place, click on and listen to the whole rhyme. Discuss the silent letters and the rhythm of the verse.
- Divide the class into two groups. Point to a place on the flashcard map and invite one group to say the name of the town or city. The other half can then say what the weather is there. Click on the map to check their answers. This can then be done in pairs.
- You can also play this game as a competition. One child from each group stands at the front of the class and they race to complete your sentence: ***Quel temps fait-il à Paris ?*** for example. The first one to say the correct weather phrase gets a point.
- Play 'Secret signal' (see page 5) with lines from the rhyme.

Core activities

- Show the class a compass and introduce the directional vocabulary.
- Agree which direction is north in your classroom and then play ***Le vent souffle du nord***. To do this, the whole class stands and you say ***Le vent souffle du nord*** (***du sud/de l'est/de l'ouest***). The children have to turn to the correct compass point as quickly as they can. The last three or four to turn are eliminated each time until there are only two or three children left standing.
- Make up sentences based on a map of France or 'Interactive flashcard: ***Quel temps fait-il à Blois ?***' For example, ***Bordeaux est dans le nord de la France***. The children must say if they are ***vrai*** (true) or ***faux*** (false). Play '***Répétez si c'est vrai***'. (See page 5 for an explanation of how to play the game.) You can also begin a sentence and challenge the children to complete it. For example, ***Bordeaux est dans ... le sud-ouest de la France***. They can then use these techniques with a partner.
- Play a guessing game. Start by saying ***je pense à une ville*** (I'm thinking of a town). The children must use the flashcard map to ask about the weather or location in order to work out which town you have chosen. For example, ***C'est dans le nord ? Il fait beau ?***
- Give each child a copy of photocopiable page 36 (***Quel temps fait-il en Suisse ?***) to complete. Display the vocabulary to help them.
- Children can also try 'Interactive activity: ***Quel temps fait-il à Blois ?***'. For this, they need to look at the map of France and Belgium and match the weather to the city or town according to the symbols on the map, and not the rhyming pattern. Double click on the sentences to hear the French spoken.

Extension activity

- Play a memory game. Ask the children to draw a hexagon (see Key words) on their whiteboards. You can then dictate the location of a city – for example, ***Paris est dans le nord de la France*** – and challenge the children to draw in where they think it is. Check their answers with a map.

Unit 3: Nord, sud, est, ouest

Tips

The children can investigate other towns in France and Belgium and create weather charts or maps to add to the class display.

Cross-curricular ideas

Geography/art and design: To make a large map for display.

Using information from a range of sources, the children can make a class map of France with pictures and facts about the major cities and regions. The map can then be labelled in French – possibly using a French script font.

PE: To play a running game.

Play a game of 'Corners' using the place names from the rhyme on 'Interactive flashcard: *Quel temps fait-il à Blois ?*'. Label the corners of the hall or playground with some of the place names. Start by calling out a place name and challenging the children to run to that corner as quickly as they can. For a variation, call out one of the weather phrases and ask the children to run to the town that it rhymes with.

Five-minute follow-ups

- At the beginning of the day, ask the children to tell you what the weather is like in the north or south of England or France. For example, ***Aujourd'hui, dans le nord de l'Angleterre il fait froid***.
- Use the place names and weather words in this unit as the basis for a phonic mobile. Every time the children find another word that rhymes they can add it. For example, begin with ***pleut*** and ***Dreux*** and then add ***bleu*** and so on.

Key words

Core:

le nord – the north
le sud – the south
l'est – the east
l'ouest – the west
le centre – the centre
le Midi – area in the south-east of France
dans – in

Extension:

le nord-est – the north-east
le nord-ouest – the north-west
le sud-est – the south-east
le sud-ouest – the south-west
l'hexagone (m) – the hexagon (France is sometimes referred to in this way due to its shape)
la boussole – the compass
aujourd'hui – today

Key phrases

Core:

il neige – it's snowing
il gèle – it's freezing
il pleut – it's raining
il fait froid – it's cold
il fait chaud – it's warm/hot
il fait beau – it's fine weather
il fait mauvais – it's bad weather
il fait gris – it's grey
le vent souffle du nord/sud – the wind is blowing from the north/south
... du nord-est – ...from the north-east
... du sud-est – ...from the south-east
... du nord-ouest – ...from the north-west
... du sud-ouest – ...from the south-west
C'est dans le sud/nord/centre ? – Is it in the south/north/centre?
... est dans le sud/nord/centre – ... is in the south/north/centre
... de la France/la Belgique – ...of France/Belgium (feminine countries)

Extension:

... de l'Angleterre – of England

Language points

- In French, the final consonant is not normally pronounced (for example, ***pleut, chaud, froid, mauvais***) except when followed by a vowel or silent 'h'. There are exceptions, however. For example, the '***-st***' in ***ouest*** and ***est*** (east) is sounded.
- When you say 'in' with names of cities and towns you use ***à*** – for example, ***à Paris***. The exception is where the name of the town includes the word ***le*** – for example, ***Le Mont Saint-Michel***. In this case, the ***à*** and ***le*** combine to become ***au*** – ***au Mont Saint-Michel***.
- When you are saying 'from the north' or 'south' use ***du*** – ***du nord, du sud*** – but use ***de l'*** for east and west as they begin with vowels – ***de l'est, de l'ouest***.

Unit 4: Les mois et les saisons

Objectives

To understand and say the months of the year in French; to understand and say the seasons and which months occur in which seasons; to learn about some of the cultural events that happen throughout the year in France.

Introducing the vocabulary

- Use 'Interactive flashcard: ***Les mois 1***' and 'Interactive flashcard: ***Les mois 2***' to introduce the months. Say to the children: ***Voici les mois de l'année*** (Here are the months of the year). Click on and listen to the months and check that the children understand. Then ask the children to listen and repeat them one month at a time.
- Introduce the seasons using 'Interactive flashcard: ***Les saisons***'. Show the children the pictures and say: ***Ce sont les quatre saisons*** (These are the four seasons). Ask them to guess what the flashcard is about. Click on the labels to hear the season words. Ask the children to listen then repeat each one. Click on each tree to hear the months in each season. Check the children have understood and then repeat.

Core activities

- Practise saying the months in French to the tune of Hickory Dickory, Dock.
- Make reading cards for the months and hand them out randomly to children. Ask the children to rearrange themselves to stand in correct month order. Ask them what they notice about how the months are written. (The lower-case initial letters.)
- Give four children each a season card. Hand out the month cards to others and ask them to stand with the correct season. Practise the vocabulary and ask children for their observations. (Many French months are very like their English equivalents. The *'ll'* in ***juillet*** may be a surprise. There is a strange mark (accent) in ***août***.)
- Explain and discuss the illustrations on 'Interactive flashcard: ***Les mois 1***' and 'Interactive flashcard: '***Les mois 2***'
  janvier – the ***galette*** (tart or cake) is the traditional dessert for ***la fête des Rois*** (Epiphany, 6 January). Whoever finds the ***fève*** (bean, usually a tiny porcelain figure) in their slice of ***galette*** is king or queen and wears the paper crown.
  février – Mardi Gras (Shrove Tuesday), a time of carnival in many European countries.
  mars – lots of French children enjoy Easter eggs or a chocolate rabbit (***un lapin en chocolat***) at ***Pâques*** (Easter).
  avril – ***poisson d'avril***. French children traditionally stick paper ***poissons*** (fish) to each other's backs as an April Fool.
  mai – ***le muguet*** (lily of the valley) has become associated with ***la fête du travail*** (May Day or Festival of Work).
  juin – ***la fête de la musique***. Both the music and cherry (***les cerises***) festivals occur in June.
  juillet – France's national day (***le 14 juillet***) is always marked with fireworks and dancing. It commemorates the storming of the ***Bastille*** prison in Paris during the French Revolution.
  août – traditional holiday month in France.
  septembre – ***la rentrée*** (the return to school).
  octobre – 31 October is ***la veille de la Toussaint*** (All Souls Day) in the church calendar, but Halloween is becoming very popular in France.
  novembre – ***l'automne*** (autumn).
  décembre – ***Noël*** (Christmas).
- Challenge groups of children to complete 'Interactive activity: ***C'est en quelle saison ?***'

Extension activities

- Practise the question and answer: ***C'est quand ton anniversaire ?*** – When is your birthday? (***Mon anniversaire, c'est en***) ***février*** – (My birthday is in) February. If children already know numbers to 31 they can give a fuller answer: ***le 2 janvier ; le vingt-quatre avril*** and so on.

Resources

Interactive flashcards:
Les mois 1
Les mois 2
Les saisons

Interactive activity:
C'est en quelle saison ?

Photocopiable page 37:
Mon calendrier

Preparation

Make a copy of Photocopiable page 37: ***Mon calendrier*** on thin A4 card for each child.

Sheets of card for each child to make their own birthday markers for a calendar.

You may wish to make your own flashcards for the months and seasons.

Interactive whiteboard

Tips

Make a wall calendar for your classroom and make this part of your daily class routine. Ask the children: ***C'est quel jour aujourd'hui ?*** (What day is it today?) and ***C'est quel mois ?*** (Which month is it?)

- If children know weather phrases, ask them about the weather in different seasons and months: ***Quel temps fait-il en été ? Quel temps fait-il en hiver/en janvier/en juillet ?***

Cross-curricular ideas

D&T: To make a personal desk calendar.

Using photocopiable page 37 (***Mon calendrier***), children can make their own simple calendars to keep on their tables to remind them of the months and seasons. They can design and make a birthday marker for their own birthday and for friends and family. These can be attached to the correct month on the calendar with a glue stick or similar. If you feel confident in giving instructions in French, tell the children: ***Prenez des ciseaux*** (Take a pair of scissors). ***Découpez le calendrier***. (Cut out the calendar). ***Pliez …*** (Fold…) ***la ligne brisée*** (the dotted line). ***Coloriez*** (Colour in). ***Découpez et décorez les étiquettes*** (Cut out the (birthday) labels). ***Attachez les étiquettes*** (Attach the labels).

Five-minute follow-ups

- Say a sequence of two or three months and ask the children to give you the next one.
- Say a season and ask the children to give you the months in that season: ***L'hiver … quels sont les mois de l'hiver ?***
- Give out the month flashcards. The child with the ***janvier*** card should start by saying their month, closely followed by the other children saying their months in order. Repeat the activity seeing how accurately and quickly they can say all twelve.

Key words

Core:

janvier – January
février – February
mars – March
avril – April
mai – May
juin – June
juillet – July
août – August
septembre – September
octobre – October
novembre – November
décembre – December
les mois (m) – the months
les saisons (f) – the seasons
quatre – four
l'année (f) – the year
le printemps – the spring
l'été (m) – the summer
l'automne (m) – the autumn
l'hiver (m) – the winter
voilà – there is/are

Key phrases

Core:

C'est en quelle saison ? – What season is it in?
en hiver – in winter
en été – in summer
en automne – in autumn
au printemps – in spring

Extension:

Ce sont … – these are…
les mois d'hiver – the months of winter
les mois d'été – the months of summer
les mois d'automne – the months of autumn
les mois de printemps – the months of spring
C'est quand, ton anniversaire ? – When is your birthday?
Mon anniversaire, c'est en février – My birthday is in February

Language points

- In French, the months, like the days of the week, are written with a lower-case first letter.
- Notice that when talking about the seasons, the French say ***en été***, ***en hiver***, ***en automne***, but ***au printemps***.

Unit 5: Mets ton chapeau !

Objectives

To learn clothes vocabulary and say what clothes they are putting on; to say which clothes they put on for different weather conditions.

Resources

Interactive flashcards: ***Mets ton chapeau ! 1*** ***Mets ton chapeau ! 2***

Interactive activity: ***Qu'est-ce que je mets ?***

Photocopiable page 38: ***Mes vêtements***

Film: ***Mets ton chapeau !***

Film transcript: ***Mets ton chapeau !***

Preparation

Make a set of cards and a spinner from photocopiable page 38: ***Mes vêtements*** for each pair or small group of children.

You may wish to make your own sets of large or small reading cards to match the picture cards.

A selection of items of clothing (optional).

Interactive whiteboard

Introducing the vocabulary

- Show the children the 'Interactive flashcard: ***Mets ton chapeau ! 1***' and click on the girl to hear the introductory sentences: ***Je passe le weekend à la plage. Qu'est-ce que je mets dans mon sac ?*** Ask the children to guess what the girl is doing and where she is going. You may have to give them ***la plage*** (the beach).
- Introduce the clothes a few at a time. Some are cognates (they sound and look like English words) so will be easy to remember. Encourage the children to point to the relevant part of their bodies or use a physical response when they say the words to reinforce memorisation. For example, they could do a swimming action for ***un maillot de bain*** or move their feet for ***des sandales***.
- Repeat the process with the 'Interactive flashcard: ***Mets ton chapeau ! 2***'.

Core activities

- Use the playing cards on photocopiable page 38 (***Mes vêtements***) to practise the clothes vocabulary. Give groups of children two sets of cards and ask them to shuffle them and spread them out on the table to play ***Le jeu de paires*** (Pelmanism). Children should say the item of clothing as they turn over each card.
- Play a game of ***Loto à deux*** (Pair bingo) for additional listening practice. Give each pair of children a set of clothes cards. They must choose six cards and turn them face up. Call out items of clothing in French and ask the children to turn over their cards as they hear them called. The first pair to turn over all six cards shouts ***Loto !***
- Ensure that the children are familiar with the weather phrases from Unit 1. Introduce and use: ***Quand*** plus a weather phrase plus ***je mets*** plus an item of clothing.
- Show the children 'Interactive activity: ***Qu'est-ce que je mets ?***'. Click on the items of clothing to hear the French and then decide which items suit which weather. As the children place the correct items, encourage them to complete the sentences, for example: ***Quand il fait froid, je mets des bottes.***
- Use items of clothing or picture cards to demonstrate the new phrases. For example, ***Quand il fait froid, je mets un chapeau/un pull.***
- Encourage the children to practise saying ***quand***. Now show them the weather flashcards (see photocopiable page 34 (***Par tous les temps***)) and put ***quand*** together with weather phrases: ***Quand il fait froid*** ... ; ***Quand il pleut*** ...and so on. Ask the children to create their own phrases as you show them the weather cards.
- Put a weather flashcard with a clothes flashcard and invite the children to make a sentence.
- Give pairs or small groups of children a set of the playing cards and a weather spinner from photocopiable page 38 (***Mes vêtements***). They must spin the spinner and pick up a card, then use what they get to make a sentence. Encourage them to consider whether the combinations are sensible.

Extension activities

- If the children are familiar with the notion of the gender of French nouns, you may wish to encourage them to use ***mon/ma/mes*** instead of ***un/une/des***.
- Watch the 'Film: ***Mets ton chapeau !*** ...' to see what you would wear if it was raining. Don't expect the children to translate all the dialogue but see whether they can tell you the date and the temperature as well as the names of the clothes the man would wear if it were raining.

Unit 5: Mets ton chapeau !

Tips

Laminate photocopied card games before cutting them up. They will last much longer.

Cross-curricular ideas

Science: To investigate the properties of materials.
Link these activities to science lessons on materials. *Why do we wear certain clothes in wet or cold weather? How do they help to protect us? Why are winter clothes often made from wool and summer clothes made from cotton?*

Five-minute follow-ups

- Make reading cards to match the clothes picture cards so that children can play Pelmanism with words and pictures and become familiar with the relationships between the spellings and sounds of the words.
- As you reveal the written words through the flashcards, discuss with the children why some words are so similar to English words. For example, ***des baskets*** has no doubt come from the popularity of basketball in the US. Look also at more challenging words like ***maillot***. Ask the children to make the sound of the letters in this word. *Which sound is made by the letters 'aill'?* (Aye.) *What do you notice about the letter 't'?* (It is silent.)
- If part of your daily class routine is to keep a French weather chart, encourage the children routinely to tell you about suitable clothes for the day's weather. Ask them: ***Quel temps fait-il aujourd'hui ?*** Once you have an answer, ask: ***Il fait froid. Qu'est-ce que tu mets, Helen ? Qu'est-ce que tu mets, Harpreet ?***

Key words

Core:

un anorak – an anorak
des baskets (m) – trainers
des bottes (f) – boots
une casquette – a cap
un chapeau – a hat
une écharpe – a scarf
une jupe – a skirt
des lunettes (f) ***de soleil*** – sunglasses
un maillot de bain – a swimsuit
des mitaines (f) – mittens
un pantalon – a pair of trousers
un pull – a jumper
des sandales (f) – sandals
un short – a pair of shorts
un sweat – a sweatshirt
un T-shirt – a T-shirt
quand – when
le weekend – the weekend
la plage – the beach

Extension:

un manteau – a coat
un parapluie – an umbrella
mon/ma/mes – my
mon sac – my bag

Key phrases

Core:

je passe – I spend/am spending (time)
je vais en montagne – I am going to the mountains
faire du ski – to ski
je mets – I put on
Qu'est-ce que je mets ... ? – What do I put on/am I putting on...?
... quand il fait beau – when the weather is fine
... quand il fait mauvais – when the weather is bad
... quand il pleut – ...when it rains
... quand il neige – ...when it snows

Language points

- ***Quand*** can be used both to ask when and to say when. We are using it here as a conjunction. For example: ***Qu'est-ce que je mets quand il fait beau ?***
- ***je mets*** comes from the verb ***mettre*** – to put/to put on (clothes).
- ***Mon, ma*** and ***mes*** are possessive adjectives. Like other adjectives in French, they must 'agree' with the gender and number of the noun. Choose the masculine form – ***mon*** – for masculine words (for example, ***mon pantalon***), the feminine form – ***ma*** – for feminine words (***ma jupe***) and the plural form for plural words (***mes bottes***). Be careful though. Words that begin with a silent 'h' or a vowel generally take the masculine form so that the sound of the language flows more easily – for example, ***mon écharpe***.

Unit 6: Au Sénégal

Objectives

To look for information in both spoken and written texts; to learn that French is spoken in countries other than France (*Sénégal*).

Introducing the vocabulary

- Before you show the children photocopiable page 39 (***Le baobab d'Afrique***), use a picture of a tree to introduce the children to the following vocabulary: ***c'est un arbre*** – it's a tree; ***les feuilles*** – the leaves; ***le tronc*** – the trunk; ***les graines*** – the seeds.

Core activities

- Show the children the 'Interactive flashcard: ***Bienvenue au Sénégal !***' Before clicking the hot spots, ask them where in the world this picture might be. What clues can they see? (The type of landscape/terrain, animals, weather.)
- Click on each hot spot starting with ***Nini***. She tells us her name and age. Click on the hut to find out where she lives. Click on the sun to hear about the weather. Finally, click on the tree to hear about the seasons. As you listen, ask the children for information about ***Nini*** and where she lives, but don't ask them to translate.
- Listen to the audio again, this time asking for specific words. Ask them to put up their hands if they hear: a number (***neuf***); any weather phrases (***chaud/il fait très chaud*** ; ***soleil*** ; ***il pleut***); or any months or seasons (***juin***, ***octobre***, ***novembre***, ***mai***, ***le printemps***, ***l'automne***).
- Can they work out what ***Il n'y a pas de printemps ni d'automne*** means? What does it mean not to have spring or autumn? (Because it is always hot in this part of Africa, which is relatively close to the Equator, there are only two seasons – wet and dry.) So what does ***De juin à octobre***, ***c'est la saison de pluie***. ***Il pleut beaucoup*** mean? Can they guess? (From June to October, it's the rainy season. It rains a lot.)
- Ask the class why the girl in this activity is speaking in French. Explain that French is spoken in more than 50 countries around the world. Do they know of any others?
- Introduce the 'Interactive activity: ***C'est où ?***' by telling the children about Quebec. Do they know where it is? Explain that Quebec is a region of Canada where people speak French but that it is very different to Senegal. Question children about Senegal and Quebec. Double click on the sentences to hear them spoken. This interactive activity can either be completed now or after Unit 7: ***Au Québec***.

Resources

Interactive flashcard: ***Bienvenue au Sénégal !***

Interactive activity: ***C'est où ?***

Photocopiable page 39: ***Le baobab d'Afrique***

Translation: ***Le baobab d'Afrique***

Preparation

Atlases and/or map of Africa

Interactive whiteboard

Extension activities

- Give each child a copy of photocopiable page 39 (***Le baobab d'Afrique***). Explain that you want them to work with a partner to see how much they can find out about the ***le baobab d'Afrique***. They should imagine that the tree is talking to them and telling them facts about himself. The ***baobab*** is called the 'tree of life', because it plays such a rich part in African culture and mythology. It is often the centre of village life, where meetings are held, and may serve as a lookout post and a storehouse for a variety of things including livestock. Almost every part of the tree is used for food or medicinal purposes. It is called '***l'arbre sens dessus dessous***' (the upside-down tree) because it appears (and legend has it) that is has been planted roots uppermost.
- Explain also the meaning of ***je peux*** – I can; ***vous pouvez*** – you can.

Cross-curricular ideas

Geography: To learn about the weather and seasons in an African country.
Ask the children to use an atlas to find Senegal on a map of Africa and to use reference books and the internet to do further research into this fascinating country.

Tips

Encourage children to discuss and share how they sometimes manage to work out the meanings of new French words for themselves. This will help them to develop language learning strategies.

Unit 6: Au Sénégal

Literacy: To write a short story or poem.
Use the ***baobab*** tree as the starting point for some creative writing. Invite the children to imagine that something – a person or creature – is living in the branches of the tree or in a hole in its trunk. *Is it friendly or frightening? What do the villagers do?* Have the children write a short poem or piece of descriptive writing following the class discussion.

Art and design: To design a fantastic, multi-purpose tree.
Encourage the children to use their imaginations to paint or draw an amazing tree that could be used for many different purposes. What would they hide in it? How would they use the flowers, seeds, leaves and bark?

Five-minute follow-ups

- Spend a few minutes each week, when the class is gathered together, to look up other francophone countries and their flags in the atlas. Discuss what the weather might be like in those countries, what might grow there and so on.
- During a PE lesson, play 'Corners' with the names of francophone countries as children become more familiar with them. If the children are familiar with the national flags and colours, increase the challenge by calling out colour combinations of the flags instead of the country name.
- Encourage the children to make up their own rap using the names of Francophone countries and their capitals.

Key words

Core:

bienvenue – welcome
le Sénégal – Senegal
l'ouest (m) – the west
l'Afrique (f) – Africa
le printemps – the spring
l'automne (m) – the autumn
la saison sèche – the dry season
la saison de(s) pluie(s) – the rainy season
un arbre – a tree
l'écorce (f) – the bark
les graines (f) – the seeds
les feuilles (f) – the leaves

Extension:

toujours – always/still
plus de – more than
par an – per year
mon/ma/mes – my
faire – to make/to do
manger – to eat
garder – to keep/guard
des médicaments (m) – medicines
un mouton – a sheep
une chèvre – a goat

Key phrases

Core:

j'habite – I live
au Sénégal – in/to Senegal
il fait chaud – it's warm/hot
il pleut – it rains
j'ai neuf ans – I am nine years old
il n'y pas de printemps ni d'automne – there is neither spring nor autumn
il pleut beaucoup – it rains a lot

Extension:

nous avons – we have
je peux – I can
vous pouvez – you can

Language points

- How we say 'in' or 'to' a country depends on the gender of the country in French. Because it is ***le Sénégal*** (masculine) we say ***au Sénégal***. Similarly with ***le Portugal* – *au Portugal* ; *le Canada* – *au Canada* ; *le Luxembourg* – *au Luxembourg***. Many countries, however, are feminine – for example: ***La France***. In this case we use ***en*** to mean 'in' or 'to' – ***en France***, ***en Suisse***, ***en Italie***, ***en Australie***, ***en Angleterre***.

Unit 7: Au Québec

Objectives

To look for information in both spoken and written texts; to learn that French is spoken in countries other than France (Canada).

Resources

Interactive flashcard: ***L'hiver au Québec***

Interactive activity: ***Au Québec***

Photocopiable page 40: ***Les animaux de la forêt québécoise***

Translation: ***Les animaux de la forêt québécoise***

Preparation

Coloured marker pens or pencils

Atlases

Simple French-English dictionaries

Interactive whiteboard

Introducing the vocabulary

- The activities in this unit focus on listening and reading for information, so vocabulary is not introduced in a formal way.

Core activities

- Approach this listening activity as a puzzle to be solved together rather than a test. Show the children 'Interactive flashcard: ***L'hiver au Québec***'. Ask them to anticipate the content of this unit from the pictures. (Some children may recognise the Canadian flag and may know that Canada is a country that is part of North America.) Look at the title. Explain that Quebec is a province of Canada. What season will they hear described?
- Click on each of the hot spots and ask the children to listen carefully and gather as much information as they can. *How old is Joseph?* (10.) *Where does he live?* (Montreal, Quebec – write up these names for later. Note that ***Montréal*** means 'royal mount or hill' and may be derived from the three-headed ***Mont Royal*** hill in the centre of the city.) *Which languages are spoken in Quebec?* (English and French.) *What is the weather like in Quebec?* (In summer, good and sunny; in winter, cold and snowy – sometimes 3m of snow.) *What kind of countryside would they see in Quebec?* (Mountains, rivers, lakes and forests.) Ask for any other details, but don't labour or explain if children have not understood all of the passage. (In summer Joseph likes fishing and walks in the mountains; in winter, tobogganing, skiing and dog-sledging.)
- Give each child a copy of photocopiable page 40 (***Les animaux de la forêt québécoise***). Ask the children to work in pairs to puzzle out this information sheet. Discuss the title first so they understand the context. Give them 10 minutes to find out as much as they can about these animals. They can use different coloured highlighter pens or coloured pencils to highlight: words they know already; words they can guess from a picture clue (***le castor***, ***le caribou***, ***les bois***, ***l'ours***); and cognates – words they can guess because they look like English words (***l'Amérique***, ***nord***, ***plantes***, ***fruits***, ***insectes***, ***attaquer***). Bring everyone back together to share what they have found out. Give lots of praise for all solutions and talk about the strategies the children have used.
- Having completed the previous activities, children can complete 'Interactive activity: ***Au Québec***', a true/false (***vrai/faux***) quiz. More confident learners may do this independently; alternatively, use it as a group or class whiteboard activity.

Extension activities

- Give the children who finish the information search above an extra challenge. Write out a list of sentences taken from the photocopiable page and see if the children can match them to the correct animal. For example, ***je construis des barrages*** ; ***j'habite dans la toundra*** ; ***j'ai des bois sur la tête***. They can also use dictionaries to find the meanings of difficult words.
- If the children have already completed Unit 6 (***Au Sénégal***) they could then attempt 'Interactive: ***C'est où ?*** which asks the children questions about ***Sénégal*** and ***Québec***.

Tips

Make a changing display in your classroom about French-speaking countries (*les pays francophones*) with the title *On parle français ...* (*au Québec/au Sénégal*).

Cross-curricular ideas

Geography: To learn about the weather and seasons, landscape and wildlife in Quebec.
Use atlases to locate Canada in the world and to find Quebec in Canada. Encourage the children to create a class book of the information they find out about Quebec. They can also make comparisons with their own locality and (if applicable) with Senegal (see Unit 6).

Science: To study animals and their habitats.
Invite the children to find out about other animals that are native to Canada, for example, where they live, what they eat and so on.

Literacy: To write a letter to a penfriend overseas.
Ask the children to imagine that they are writing a letter to Joseph, the boy featured in 'Interactive flashcard: *L'hiver au Québec*'. They can include (in French) their name, age, where they live and an activity they enjoy (see Unit 2).

Five-minute follow-ups

- Make large format text cards for a selection of words and phrases learned through this unit, such as *au Québec ; il y a ; des forêts ; des montagnes ; des lacs ; des rivières ; il neige ; en hiver ; il fait beau ; en été ; des castors ; des caribous ; des ours noirs*. Ask the children to use the cards to make different sentences.
- Encourage the children to use *il y a* (there is/there are) with any familiar language in different contexts. Ask: *Qu'est-ce qu'il y a dans la photo/dans la salle de classe ?* (What is there in the photo/the classroom?) and so on.

Key words

Core:

le Québec – Quebec
français – French
anglais – English
un pays – a country
une montagne – a mountain
une forêt – a forest
une rivière – a river
un lac – a lake
la toundra – the tundra
le castor – the beaver
le caribou – caribou
le renne – reindeer
l'ours (m) *noir* – the black bear
les dents (f) – teeth
les bois (m) – antlers (also means woods)

Extension:

souvent – often
beaucoup (*de*) – lots (of)

Key phrases

Core:

il y a – there is/there are
on parle – one speaks/they speak
je parle – I speak
manger – to eat
il mange – he/it eats
couper – to cut
il coupe – he/it cuts
nager – to swim
il nage – he/it swims
dormir – to sleep
il dort – he/it sleeps
les dents puissantes – strong teeth
un pelage long et épais – a long thick coat
faire du toboggan – to go tobogganing
faire une promenade – to go for a walk
faire une randonnée – to go for a hike/go hiking

Extension:

en traîneau à chiens – by dog-sledge
plus de – more than

Language points

- Literally, *on* is the equivalent of the English pronoun 'one', but it does not have connotations of 'high register' language. In French *on* is used very frequently because it is quicker than using the *nous* form of the verb – for example, *On va au cinéma ?* (Shall we go to the cinema?)
- Note that, unusually, the final 's' in *ours* is sounded. You may remember this by thinking of Ursa Minor – the Little Bear constellation.

Unit 8: Le cycle de l'eau

Objectives

To practise reading skills; to understand that other languages have the same conventions of style and layout; to use language learned in one context in another.

Introducing the vocabulary

- Show the children 'Interactive flashcard: ***Le cycle de l'eau***'. Ask them if they can think of any weather language or water cycle vocabulary that will be relevant to this diagram.
- Encourage the children to discuss, in English, what they remember about the water cycle.
- Look at each part of the water cycle on the flashcard together. Allow the children to listen and then ask them to suggest the meaning of each sentence. Encourage them to describe the decoding strategies they are using. Show them that on this occasion the structure of the sentence is the same as in English. Ask them to identify nouns and verbs. How does this help their understanding? What other clues are they using? (The illustrations, their prior knowledge.)

Core activities

- When the children have familiarised themselves with 'Interactive flashcard: ***Le cycle de l'eau***', they can try the sequencing exercise in 'Interactive activity: ***Le cycle de l'eau***' either as a class or in small groups. (There is a translation of the text available on the CD-ROM if required.)
- Hand out photocopiable page 41 (***Le cycle de l'eau***). Ask the children to label the diagram of the water cycle using the wordbank provided.
- Try a matching game. Give each child a sentence from the water cycle text in either English or French. They have to circulate around the room and find their partner who has the same sentence in the other language. Once everyone has found their partners, ask the whole class, staying in their pairs, to get into sequence.
- Working in small groups, the children play a memory game. Use the cards of the French sentences which you have cut into two (see Preparation). The children place these cards face down on the table and then each pick two cards. If the two halves make a sentence from the water-cycle text they keep them. Children can check their answers using the Interactive flashcard. Alternatively, read out the sentences in the correct order and have the children wave the sentences in the air as they hear them.
- If you have a series of pictures or a big picture of the water cycle, children can stick their completed sentences in the correct position to create a display.
- Encourage each group to make up some questions to ask the rest of the class. They could be true or false questions (***La vapeur d'eau*** means 'river'. True or false?), translations (How do you say...?) or a challenge to say the next sentence in the cycle. Keep these questions for later.

Resources

Interactive flashcard:
Le cycle de l'eau

Interactive activity:
Le cycle de l'eau

Translation:
Le cycle de l'eau

Photocopiable page 41:
Le cycle de l'eau

Preparation

You will also need cards of the phrases from the interactive flashcard and their English translations – for example, ***la vapeur d'eau monte dans l'air*** and 'the water vapour rises into the air' – and cards of the French sentences cut into two halves, for example, ***La vapeur d'eau*** and ***monte dans l'air*** (See Core activities.)

A big picture or pictures of the water cycle (optional)

Blu-Tack® or glue (optional)

Interactive whiteboard

Extension activities

- Introduce the extension phrases and talk about how we use water in the home. The children can make a tally chart of the number of times they use water in each of these ways in a day or week.
- More confident learners may wish to use dictionaries to find the infinitives of the verbs in the water cycle text. The verbs that end in ***-e*** or ***-ent*** in the text all belong to the ***-er*** group.

Unit 8: Le cycle de l'eau

Tips

Encourage the children to think of other occasions where they may reuse some of this language, such as ***se transforme en*** (turns into).

Key words

Core:

l'eau (f) – the water

la mer – the sea

l'océan (m) – the ocean

la rivière – the river

le lac – the lake

l'énergie (f) ***solaire*** – the sun's energy

l'évaporation (f) – the evaporation

les précipitations – the precipitation

la condensation – the condensation

les montagnes (f) – the mountains

les nuages (m) – the clouds

le vent – the wind

le soleil – the sun

la neige – the snow

la grêle – the hail

du brouillard – fog

devenir – to become

Extension:

la terre – the earth

les gouttelettes (f) – the droplets

chauffer – to heat

la chaleur – the heat

les collines (f) – the hills

Cross-curricular ideas

Drama/dance: To create a performance based on the water cycle.
Encourage the children to represent different parts of the water cycle through movement. An adult or confident child can read out the sentences as the children play the parts of the sun, river, water droplets and so on.

Music: To compose a piece based on the water cycle.
Children can experiment with instruments and choose which ones could be used to represent each stage of the water cycle. Their compositions can be added to the dance/drama performance to create a class assembly.

Maths: To present data in different ways.
Invite the children to use the information they collect about water usage to create bar charts and/or pie charts. They could also think about ways of measuring the amounts of water they use for each task.

Five-minute follow-ups

- As the children come across more ***-tion*** words, collect them together to make a sound mobile.
- Revisit the children's challenge sentences to see how much they can remember a week or so later.

Key words

la brume – the mist

se jeter – to flow (river)

la transpiration – the transpiration

Key phrases

Core:

le soleil brille – the sun shines

la neige fond – the snow melts

l'eau s'évapore – the water evaporates

la vapeur monte – the water vapour rises

la vapeur devient froide – the vapour becomes cold

Extension:

chez moi – at home

j'utilise l'eau pour ... – I use water for...

...laver les vêtements – ...washing clothes

... boire – ...drinking

... me laver les dents – ...cleaning my teeth

... préparer les repas – ...preparing meals

... faire la vaisselle – ...doing the washing-up

Language points

- Use the water cycle text to focus on the third person singular and plural of ***-er*** verbs and ***devenir*** in the present tense. Year 5 and 6 children could be asked to look for patterns.
- Work on the children's pronunciation of ***-tion*** words. Practise the sound (***tsion***) and agree on a gesture to represent it. Discuss the fact that pronunciation of this sound is always the same. Can the children think of any other examples? Words ending in ***-tion*** are usually feminine.
- For the extension task, explain to the children how to say ***j'utilise l'eau pour*** plus an infinitive (I use water to...).

Unit 9: Quel temps fait-il en Europe ?

Objectives

To understand and use the names for francophone countries in Europe; to understand and use the vocabulary for some European languages/nationalities; to consolidate language for geographical features.

Resources

Interactive flashcard: ***On parle français en Europe***

Interactive activity: ***On parle français en Europe***

Photocopiable page 42: ***Quel temps fait-il en Europe ?***

Preparation

Mini whiteboards and pens (optional)

Interactive whiteboard

Introducing the vocabulary

- Show the children 'Interactive flashcard: ***On parle français en Europe***' and ask them to tell you any information they can (in English or French) about the countries featured on the map.
- Click on the names of the countries and practise the pronunciation of these words with the children. Ensure they know their meanings.
- Now click on ***Anouk***'s picture. Give the children a few minutes to read the sentences about her. Working in pairs using mini whiteboards, encourage them to jot down the English translations of any words they already know. They can then divide the other side of their whiteboard into two sections – one for their guesses for words they don't already know and the other for their reasons for each guess.
- Discuss the language learning strategies the children used to discover meaning and share the new vocabulary in this text.

Core activities

- Continue to study 'Interactive flashcard: ***On parle français en Europe***' using a different focus for each section of text.
- ***Armand*** : Encourage the children to guess the content of the text and note down phrases in English which they think might appear. Award points for each correct guess. At this point, there is no need to translate every word.
- ***Sylvie*** : This time, ask the children to say sentences in French that they think might appear in the text, before you click to check.
- ***Natalie*** : Show the children the text and ask simple comprehension questions in English: *What's her name?* and so on.
- ***Roman*** : Now ask comprehension questions in French: ***Comment s'appelle-t-il ?*** for example.
- Divide the class into three teams: Team 1 = languages, Team 2 = countries, Team 3 = geographical features. Read or highlight a sentence from one of the hot spots and ask the teams to listen out for examples of their type of words. They have to say how many times one of their words appears in each sentence. Award points for the children who get the correct number, with bonus points if they can say their words in French.
- Choose a volunteer to come out to the front and pretend to be one of the children in the flashcard. They have to say a sentence – for example, ***je parle français*** – and the rest of the class have to guess who he or she is. This can be extended so that the children have to ask questions to the volunteer: ***Tu habites au bord d'un lac ?*** and so on.
- The children can then work through 'Interactive activity: ***On parle français en Europe***'.
- Finally, ask the children to look back at the interactive flashcard and identify the French-speaking countries and any other information they can remember from these activities.
- On photocopiable page 42 (***Quel temps fait-il en Europe ?***), the same European children tell us about the weather where they live. Challenge your class to answer the questions and then ask them to say what the weather is like in summer and winter where they live. (***Et là où vous habitez ? En été ... ; En hiver ...***)

Cross-curricular ideas

Geography: To find out about a European country.
Invite the children to use atlases, reference books and the internet to find out more about the geographical features of French-speaking Europe.

Unit 9: Quel temps fait-il en Europe ? 

Tips

The circumflex (ˆ) replaces the letter '*s*' in old French. Children can make a collection of words they find with this accent and work out their meanings. For example, *une île* – an island.

Literacy: To write a persuasive text.
Children can design a poster to attract tourists to their chosen French-speaking country. They should include some of the facts they have learned about the country together with reasons why people would want to visit there. More experienced children could combine this with bilingual dictionary work and produce a bilingual or French poster.

History: To study famous people and events.
Challenge the children to find out about a famous person or historical event that is linked with each of the countries featured on 'Interactive flashcard: *On parle français en Europe*'.

Five-minute follow-ups

- Over the course of a week, invite the children to monitor the weather for each of the countries studied and produce a chart. At the end of the week they can decide which country they would prefer to have spent the week in and explain why.
- Go back to the interactive flashcard and re-read the text, highlighting any language not already addressed. Ask extension questions about the countries – for example, ***Quelle est la capitale de la France ?***

Key words

Core:

la France – France
la Suisse – Switzerland
la Belgique – Belgium
l'Andorre (f) – Andorra
la Corse – Corsica
une rivière – a river
un lac – a lake
une île – an island
le français – French
l'anglais (m) – English
le flamand – Flemish
l'italien (m) – Italian
l'allemand (m) – German
le catalan – Catalan

Extension:

les Pyrénées (f) – the Pyrenees
les Pyrénées Atlantiques – the Atlantic, used to refer to the Western Pyrenees
les Pyrénées Occidentales – the Eastern Pyrenees
la Méditerranée – the Mediterranean
l'ouest (m) – the west
plus de/d' – more than
entre – between
l'Espagne (f) – Spain
le romanche – Romansh, spoken in Switzerland
la capitale – the capital

Key phrases

Core:

je m'appelle – my name is
j'habite – I live
je parle – I speak
on parle – we speak/one speaks (see Language points in Unit 7)
un petit village –a small village
une très grande ville – a very big town

Extension:

au bord d'/de – on the edge of
au cœur des Alpes – in the heart of the Alps
il fait partie de – he/it belongs to
une très petite principauté – a very small principality

Language points

- In this unit 'in' is translated as follows: ***à*** plus the name of a town (***à Bruxelles***); ***dans*** for a type of place (***dans un village***); ***en*** plus the name of a feminine country (***en France***).
- The words for languages – for example, ***français*** – are also used as adjectives for the country. So 'I am French' – ***je suis français*** (for a boy) or ***je suis française*** (for a girl) because the adjective must agree. The feminine forms of the adjectives used in this unit are formed by adding '***e***', except for ***italienne***.

Unit 10: Quel temps fait-il aujourd'hui ?

Objectives

To revise weather vocabulary; to learn a song in French to perform; to listen for specific words and rhymes.

Introducing the vocabulary

- Use the picture cards from photocopiable page 34 (*Par tous les temps*). Show them to the children and ask them to say each weather phrase. Go around the room asking each table to pronounce the phrase – the best table wins the card. Repeat this until you have given out cards for all the weather phrases in the song (see below), ensuring that each table has at least one card (you will need *il pleut, il neige, il fait beau, il fait chaud, il fait du soleil, il fait mauvais, il fait froid* and *il fait du vent*.)
- Play the class the 'Song: *Quel temps fait-il aujourd'hui ?*'. For the first listening, ask each table to stand up as they hear their weather phrase, with one person holding up their picture card. (Note the slight variance of *le soleil brille* and *il y a du vent*.)
- For the second listening, the children have to stand up as before, but this time do an action to represent the weather phrase.
- For the third listening, the children have to stand up, do an action and sing their line. (Note that the second listening stage can be skipped if the children are very familiar with the language.)

Core activities

- Working in groups, play the children the song again and ask them to put their own set of picture cards from photocopiable page 34 (*Par tous les temps*) into the correct order.
- Now build the song back up as a class. Put the large pictures up on the board as the children say the lines of the song. Leave gaps for the question.
- Ask the children to tell you the question that they have heard in the song: *Quel temps fait-il aujourd'hui ?* Write it on the board between each set of pictures. Practise the pronunciation of this phrase by breaking it into chunks. Start by chanting the final word together and then build it back up into a full sentence.
- Divide the class into two groups – A and B. Group A has to chant the question. Show a weather picture to Group B (without Group A seeing it) and encourage them to chant back the weather phrase. Someone from Group A has to mime the weather or say it in English to show that they have understood the phrase. Award points to Group A for good pronunciation and to Group B for comprehension. Swap over and play again. For a fun variation, children can sing the phrases or say them in a funny voice.
- 'Interactive activity: *Quel temps fait-il aujourd'hui ?*' is a simple translation exercise where the children will get instant feedback on their ability to understand the weather phrases from this unit.

Resources

Interactive flashcard: *Quel temps fait-il aujourd'hui ?*

Interactive activity: *Quel temps fait-il aujourd'hui ?*

Photocopiable page 34: *Par tous les temps*

Photocopiable page 43: *Les dominos*

Photocopiable: *Quel temps fait-il aujourd'hui ?*

Song: *Quel temps fait-il aujourd'hui ?*

Translation: *Quel temps fait-il aujourd'hui ?*

Preparation

Give a copy of Photocopiable page 34: *Par tous les temps* to each group

Make large weather picture cards using images from photocopiable page 34 or photographs.

Interactive whiteboard

Extension activities

- Children can perform the song. Place a weather map or pictures on a board and ask one group of children to come forward from one side singing *Quel temps fait-il aujourd'hui ?* Another small group can come out from the other side of the board, meet them in the middle, give a reply and then go back again. Have a different group for each verse.
- Use 'Interactive flashcard: *Quel temps fait-il aujourd'hui ?*' to practise using the *il y a* construction as well as some different types of weather. Ask *Quel temps fait-il aujourd'hui ?* and encourage the children to respond using *il fait* or, where appropriate, *il y a*.

Unit 10: Quel temps fait-il aujourd'hui ?

Tips

At the beginning of each day ask the children to say or write down the weather and amend this if it changes during the day.

Cross-curricular ideas

Music: To compose a new tune for a song.
Encourage the children to try changing the tune to ***Quel temps fait-il aujourd'hui ?*** They could invent their own in different styles, such as rock and roll or rap, or put the words to a tune they already know such as a TV theme tune.

PE: To play a traditional playground game.
As a game for breaktime or a warm-up exercise, play a version of 'What's the time Mr Wolf?' using the question and answers from the song in place of the time. Before you begin, agree on the weather phrase that will be the equivalent of 'Dinnertime!'

ICT: To experiment with different fonts and effects.
Invite the children to type out one verse or the whole song using different fonts and text effects to represent different types of weather.

Five-minute follow-ups

- Using photocopiable page 43 (***Les dominos***) children can play a quick game to practise putting together the question ***Quel temps fait-il aujourd'hui ?*** and the weather phrases from the song. Encourage them to look carefully at the cards and make sure they match up the words exactly. The dominoes should be placed in the order in which the phrases appear in the song.
- Say or sing the song at lining-up time, for example. Challenge the children to change parts of the song and add their own weather vocabulary.

Key words

Core:

aussi – also/too
comme – as/like
mais – but
très – very
et – and

Key phrases

Core:

Quel temps fait-il aujourd'hui ? – What's the weather like today?
il fait beau – the weather is fine
il fait mauvais – the weather is bad
il fait du soleil – it's sunny
il fait chaud – it's warm/hot
il fait froid – it's cold
il pleut – it's raining
il neige – it's snowing
il fait du vent – it's windy
le soleil brille – the sun is shining

Extension:

il fait du brouillard – it's foggy
il fait de l'orage – it's stormy
il y a du vent – it's windy
il y a du brouillard – it's foggy
il y a du soleil – it's sunny
il y a du vent – it's windy

Language points

- So far, the weather phrases have used ***il fait*** plus an adjective – for example, ***il fait froid***. The phrase ***il y a*** can also be used with some nouns (see Key phrases, Extension). You can use either ***il y a du vent*** or ***il fait du vent***, for example.

Unit 11: Eric l'épouvantail

Objectives

To understand extended sentences in French; to practise predicting and deducing meaning from context; to manipulate language by changing an element in a sentence.

Resources

Interactive flashcard: *Eric l'épouvantail*

Interactive activity: *Eric l'épouvantail*

Photocopiable page 44: *Ecris et dessine*

Photocopiable page 34: *Par tous les temps*

Preparation

An old hat, an old pair of sunglasses, an old coat, a woollen scarf and a pair of wellington boots in a bag (other items can be included if the children have already done Unit 5)

Interactive whiteboard

Introducing the vocabulary

- Display 'Interactive flashcard: ***Eric l'épouvantail***' and introduce the scarecrow to the children. In picture 1, click on Eric's face and listen to the audio clip. Ask the children what they think ***champ de choux*** could mean. Encourage them to use their literacy skills (such as looking at the illustration) to aid their understanding.
- Invite the children to guess any words that they think the scarecrow will use to describe what he's wearing. In picture 1, click on Eric's hat and work out the meaning of the sentence together. Repeat this for pictures 2, 3 and 4 – sunglasses, scarf and coat and wellington boots). The children will be familiar with some of the clothes and weather vocabulary if you have completed Units 1 and 5.
- Encourage the children to guess which weather phrases will be associated with the items of clothing. You can then click on the sky areas of each picture to listen to the hot spots and the children can check their guesses.
- To consolidate this learning, click on each hot spot in turn and ask one half of the room to repeat the clothes and the other the weather. Swap over and repeat.

Core activities

- Now focus on the sky-area hot spots of 'Interactive flashcard: ***Eric l'épouvantail***'. Click on each of the hot spots and encourage the children, working in groups, to decide on their meaning. Ask for suggestions after each one. Discuss the language learning strategies that the children used to make their decisions.
- Take out an item of clothing from the bag and say: ***C'est mon/ma ...*** or ***Ce sont mes ...*** Encourage the children to supply the noun. Now close your eyes and invite a volunteer to take an item from the bag and hide it behind their back. You have to guess what it is by saying ***C'est mon ... ?*** and so on. The children can give you clues by saying what the appropriate weather would be for the item of clothing.
- Reverse the activity by asking the children to secretly choose a weather picture card from photocopiable page 34 (***Par tous les temps***). The teacher must then guess the weather phrase – ***il pleut***, for example. The children can prompt you by saying an item of clothing you would wear in that weather. Confident children can then take on your role.
- When all the children are familiar with the language, divide the class into two teams. Pull an item out of the bag and the first team to say the appropriate sentence from the first screen of the interactive flashcard wins a point. The team could all chant the sentence together or divide it among several children – for example, ***je porte/mes bottes/quand/il neige***. Extra points could be given if teams can add ***pour me protéger*** or if they can use additional vocabulary.
- Continue the activity by taking items from the bag which don't come from this unit and challenge the children to make a new sentence orally or write it on their whiteboards.
- 'Interactive activity: ***Eric l'épouvantail***' and photocopiable page 44 (***Ecris et dessine***) provide the children with extra practice in the vocabulary and sentence structures covered in this unit.

Extension activity

- Explore the gender of nouns and explain how this affects the choice of possessive adjective. Reinforce this by taking items out of the bag and asking the children if they should say ***mon***, ***ma*** or ***mes*** for each one.

Tips

Incorporate a ***mon/ma/mes*** section into your word wall and add items as the children meet them.

Cross-curricular ideas

Drama: To act out a story in French.

Encourage the class to create their own performance based on ***Eric l'épouvantail***, simplifying the sentences or changing items. Some children may wish to make a comedy sketch by mismatching clothes and weather. They could also develop a short play where items of clothing are given to the wrong person – perhaps set on a windy day or in a disorganised laundrette! Each person has to retrieve their own item by saying ***C'est mon/ma/mes …***

ICT: To create a labelled diagram.

Children could decide on the best tools to use to draw and label their own picture of a scarecrow or person.

Art and design: To create a photographic montage.

Encourage the children to cut out photos of clothes they like from magazines and catalogues. They can then find a suitable face and stick on pictures to 'dress' their person. They could theme their picture by choosing a single colour to use, or dress the figure for a particular type of weather or occasion.

Five-minute follow-ups

- Before the children go out to play, ask them to tell you what the weather is like and then to say what they are going to wear. For example, ***Aujourd'hui il pleut. Je porte mon/ma/mes …***
- For additional practice, pretend to steal an item of clothing and say that the child can only get it back by saying ***C'est mon …***

Key words

Core:

un épouvantail – a scarecrow
mon/ma/mes – my
ma maison – my house
un vieux chapeau – an old hat
mon chapeau – my hat
un vieux manteau – an old coat
mon manteau – my coat
une écharpe en laine – a woolly scarf
des bottes (f) *en caoutchouc* – Wellington boots
de vieilles lunettes (f) *de soleil* – old sunglasses
mes lunettes de soleil – my sunglasses
quand – when
Aïe ! – expression similar to Oh no! or Ouch!
merci – thank you

Key phrases

Core:

un champs de choux – a cabbage field
c'est – it is
ce sont – they are
je porte – I'm wearing
pour me protéger – to protect me
il fait froid – it's cold
il fait du soleil – it's sunny
il fait du vent – it's windy
il neige – it's snowing
il pleut – it's raining

Extension:

il pleut à verse – it's raining heavily
le soleil brille – the sun is shining
au secours ! – help!
s'envole – flies away

Language points

- This unit includes more work on the possessive adjectives ***mon***, ***ma*** and ***mes*** that were introduced in Unit 5. Remember that you choose which one to use depending on the gender of the noun, and not the person speaking. For example, ***mon chapeau*** (masculine), ***ma maison*** (feminine) and ***mes lunettes*** (plural). ***Mon*** is also used for feminine words that begin with a silent '***h***' or a vowel, such as ***mon écharpe*** (feminine).
- This unit may be the point at which you decide to introduce your class to the concept that all nouns in French are either masculine or feminine.

Unit 12: En colonie de vacances

Objectives

To develop their cultural understanding about similarities and differences between the lives of English and French children; to practise sentence building combining previously learned words and/or phrases; to use a writing frame to write a letter or postcard home.

Resources

Interactive flashcard: ***En colonie de vacances***

Interactive activity: ***Une carte postale***

Photocopiable page 45: ***Jeux***

Photocopiable: ***Où vas-tu passer les vacances ?***

Song: ***Où vas-tu passer les vacances ?***

Translation: ***Où vas-tu passer les vacances ?***

Preparation

Large map of France showing the points of the compass in French, seas and mountains

You will need to make text cards of the key phrases and words in this unit (see below) and picture cards showing horse-riding, skiing, walking, cycling, sandcastle building, pottery and drama

Interactive whiteboard

Introducing the vocabulary

- The activities in this unit focus on listening and reading for information, so vocabulary is not introduced in a formal way. However, you may want to use any of the flashcards from the previous units to revise vocabulary.

Core activities

- Show the children 'Interactive flashcard: ***En colonie de vacances***'. Explain that French children and teenagers often go on specially organised group holidays at ***colonies de vacances***. These are a bit like American summer camps. Tell the class that they are going to hear more about ***colonies de vacances*** and that they will hear lots of French words and phrases which they have learned previously.
- Click on the picture of a group of French children. *Which seasons are mentioned?* (***L'hiver, l'été***.) Click on the picture of skiers. *Which mountains are mentioned?* (***Les Alpes, les Pyrénées*** – check on your wall map that the children know where these are.) *What sports do the children like doing in these mountains?* (***Faire du ski/ du snowboard en hiver; faire des randonnées à pied/à cheval en été***.) Click on the seaside picture. *Which parts of France are mentioned?* (***Le sud, la Méditerranée***.) *Which season is mentioned?* (***L'été***.) Ask similar questions about each picture.
- Make a set of large text cards showing key phrases and words: ***j'aime/je n'aime pas/aller/à la plage/aux montagnes/faire/du ski/du ski nautique/du snowboard/ du théâtre/de la poterie/du vélo/à cheval/à pied/à vélo/des châteaux de sable/en été/en hiver***. First get the children to think of things they like doing ***en été***. Start by building phrases to match pictures you show them. For example, ***j'aime*** plus ***aller à la plage*** or ***j'aime*** plus ***faire du vélo***. Start with sentences about what the children like doing using ***j'aime***, then move on to using ***je n'aime pas*** to express their dislikes. Build in more complexity by adding ***en été*** or ***en hiver***. Make a human sentence – give a group of children large word cards. They must hold up the cards and assemble themselves in the correct order to make a sentence.
- Children can use the word puzzles on photocopiable page 45 (***Jeux***) to focus on spellings of words they have encountered in this and in previous units.

Extension activities

- Use 'Interactive activity: ***Une carte postale***' with the class to write a model postcard home to parents. More confident learners may be able to write their own imaginary holiday postcards home.
- Listen to the 'Song: ***Où vas-tu passer les vacances ?***'. (A translation of the lyrics is available on the CD-ROM.)

Unit 12: En colonie de vacances

Tips

Use mini whiteboards to encourage the children to write sentences and phrases. Encourage them to work in pairs and to check and correct each others' writing.

Cross-curricular ideas

ICT: To carry out online research.

Challenge the children to find out as much information as they can about ***colonies de vacances*** from websites such as **www.123sejours.com** and **www.lescolos.com**. Obviously the French on these sites will be complicated, but they should be able to get a good idea about the activities on offer from the photos and the vocabulary they already know.

PSHE/citizenship: To hold a class debate.

Using what they now know, invite the children to debate the motion: All children should spend a week of the summer holidays at a ***colonie de vacances***. Divide the class into two groups to prepare arguments for and against the motion and hold a class vote at the end.

Drama: To mime sports and activities.

Play a quick game of charades to practise the vocabulary in this unit. Volunteers must mime one of the activities for the others to guess.

Five-minute follow-ups

- For additional practice of the core activities, give pairs of children small sets of cards with which to build sentences.
- Ask the children to bring in photos or to draw or paint pictures and write captions in French to show what they like doing on holiday. Use them to gradually put together an ***En vacances*** display.

Key words

The intention of this final unit is to bring together vocabulary and structures introduced in the preceding units of this book. Since the vocabulary has already been introduced, this list focuses on words children will need to use for sentence building and then writing a letter.

Extension:

en vacances – on holiday
super – great/smashing
génial – great/smashing
cher/chère/chers – dear
bisous (m) – kisses

Key phrases

Core:

c'est – it is
j'aime – I like
je n'aime pas – I don't like
faire du ski – to ski/go skiing
faire du ski nautique – to waterski/go waterskiing
faire du snowboard – to snowboard/go snowboarding
faire une promenade – to go for a walk
faire des randonnées à cheval/à vélo – to go/going for horse/bike rides
faire de la poterie – (to do) pottery
faire du théâtre – (to do) drama
faire des châteaux de sable – to make/making sandcastles
aller à la plage – to go/going to the beach
apprendre à cuisiner – to learn/learning to cook

Extension:

tout en haut – right at the top
on peut voir – one can see/you can see
parce que – because

Language points

Remind the children of the difference between ***en*** and ***dans***. Each can mean in but we say: ***en France/en Angleterre*** for 'in France/in England', but ***dans le sud de la France*** for 'in the south of France' and ***dans le nord de l'Italie*** for 'in the north of Italy'.

Par tous les temps

il pleut

il fait du soleil

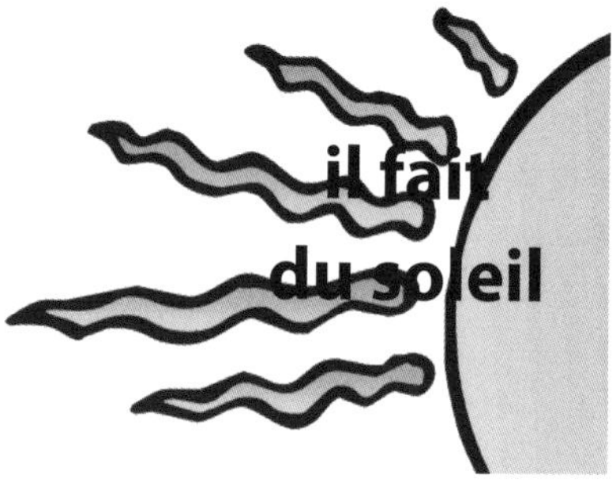

il neige

il fait chaud

il fait du vent

il fait froid

il fait du brouillard

il fait de l'orage

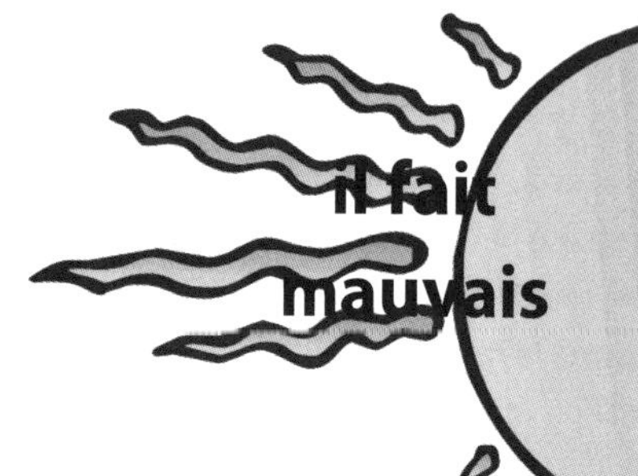

il fait mauvais

il fait beau

Quand il fait beau ...

Je m'appelle ____________________

Quand il fait beau, j'aime ____________________

____

____

Quand il fait mauvais, j'aime ____________________

____

____

Quel temps fait-il en Suisse ?

Regardez la carte et les symboles. Complétez les phrases :
Exemple: *Il pleut à Lausanne.*

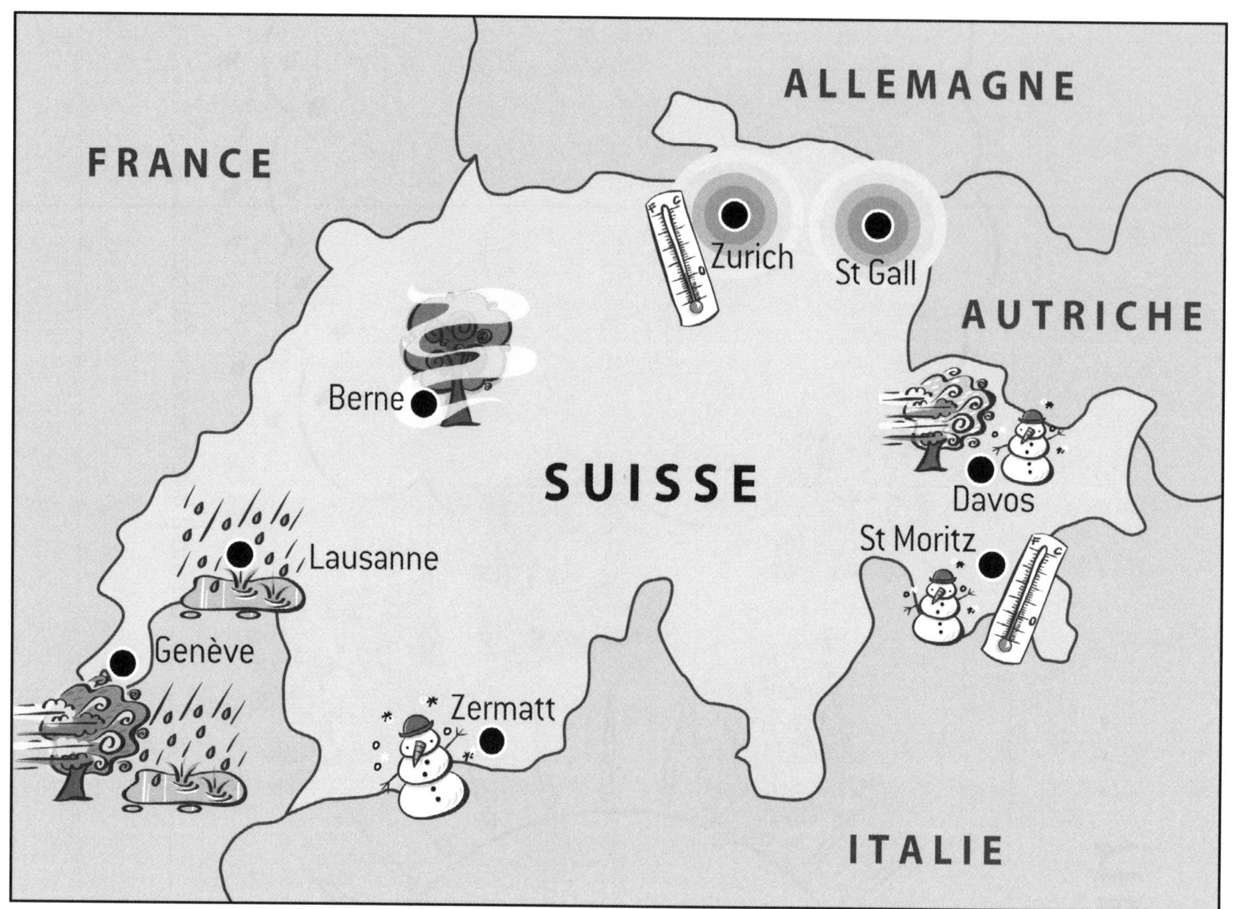

1. *A Zermatt il* ______________________________.

2. *A St Gall Il fait* ______________________________.

3. *Il* ______________ *du* ______________ *à Berne*.

4. *A Genève il* ______________ *et il* ______________.

5. *A St Moritz il* ______________ *et il* ______________.

6. *A Zürich* ______________________________.

7. *A Davos* ______________________________.

8. *Quel temps fait-il chez toi ?* (What's the weather like where you are?)

______________________________.

Mon calendrier

Réalisation du calendrier :

Décorez le calendrier selon les mois et les saisons. Par exemple, des poissons en avril, la neige en hiver.

Coloriez !

Amusez-vous bien !

How to make the calendar:

Decorate the calendar according to the months and the seasons. For example, fish in April for April Fools' day and snow in winter.

Colour!

Have fun!

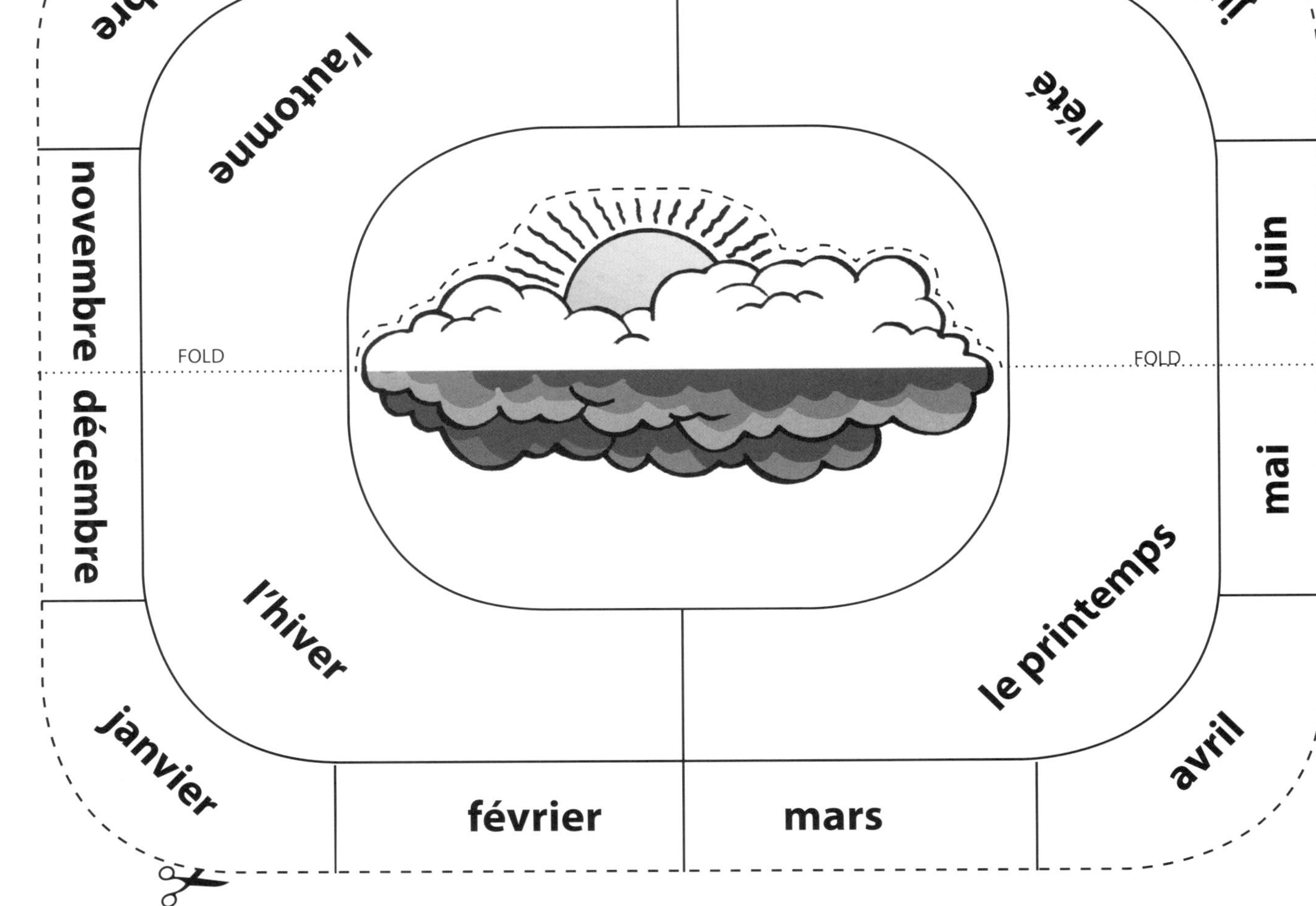

- - - - - - - - - - - = pliez (fold)

.... = coupez (cut)

Mes vêtements

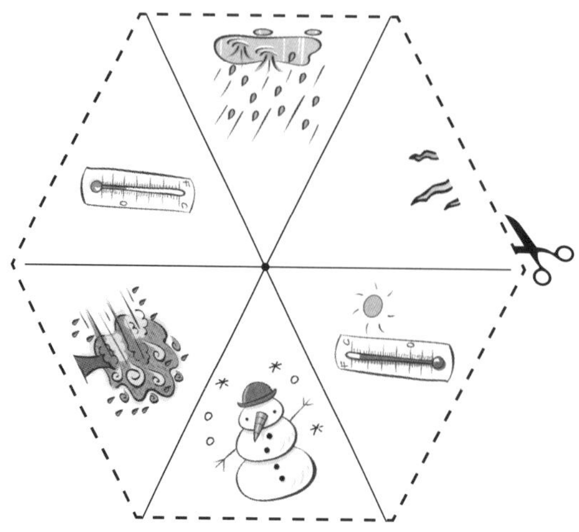

Le baobab d'Afrique

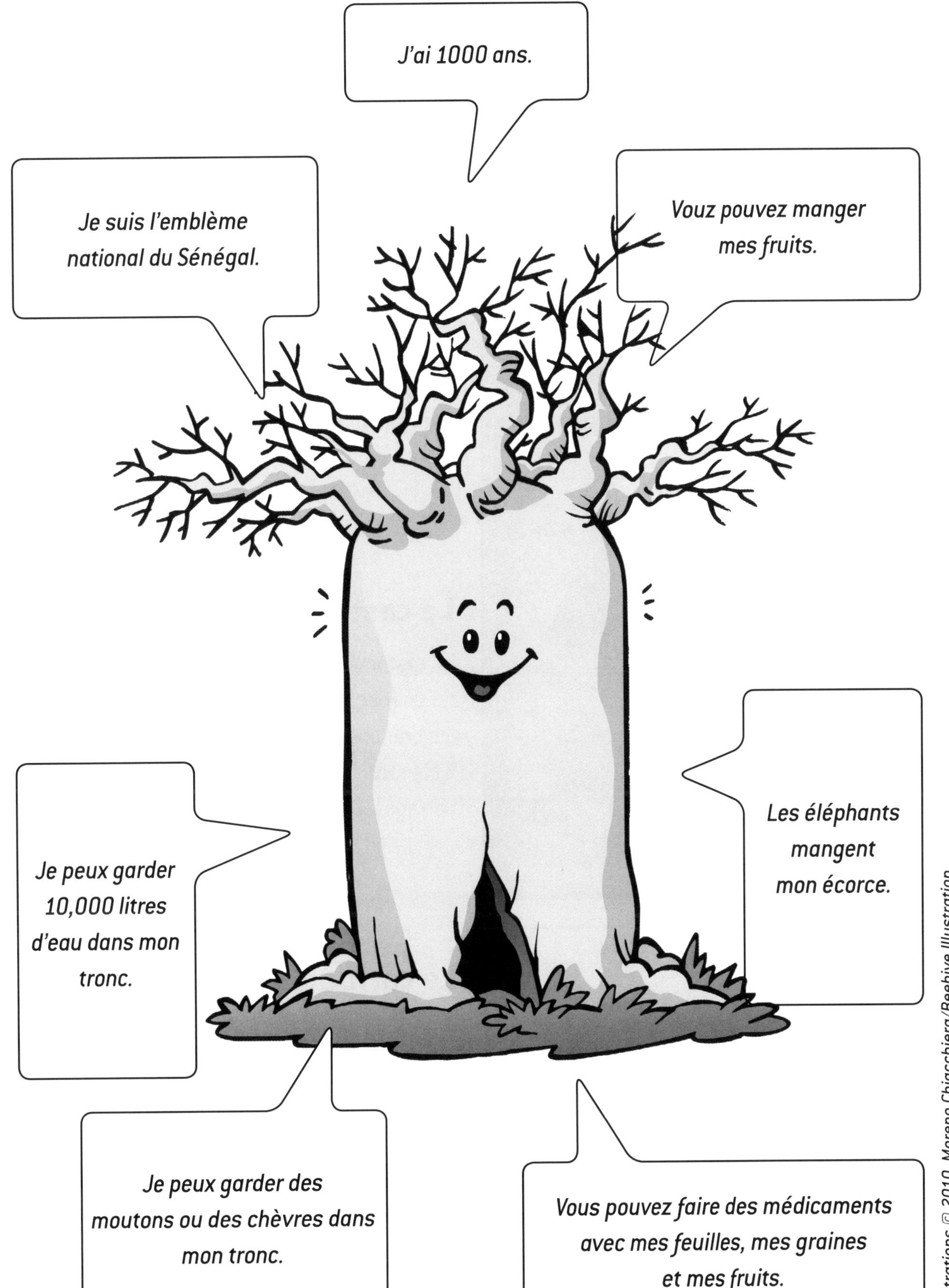

Les animaux de la forêt québécoise

L'ours noir

Il y a plus de 600,000 ours noirs dans l'Amérique du Nord. L'ours noir habite dans les forêts. Il mange tout : les plantes, les fruits, les insectes et les poissons. Attention – il peut des fois attaquer les hommes ! En hiver il ne mange pas beaucoup. Il passe beaucoup de temps à dormir.

Le castor

Le castor vit dans les forêts et les lacs du Québec. C'est un animal timide. Il coupe les branches avec ses dents puissantes. Il construit sa maison (une hutte) et des barrages. C'est un très bon nageur.

Le caribou

Un million de caribous vivent dans la toundra du Québec. En Europe ils s'appellent 'rennes'. (C'est eux qui aident à tirer le traîneau du père Noël !) Un pelage long et épais leur permet de rester chauds en hiver, même quand il neige beaucoup. Ils mangent des lichens et des plantes. Le mâle porte d'immenses bois sur la tête.

Le cycle de l'eau

Cut out the word cards and stick them in the correct places on the diagram.

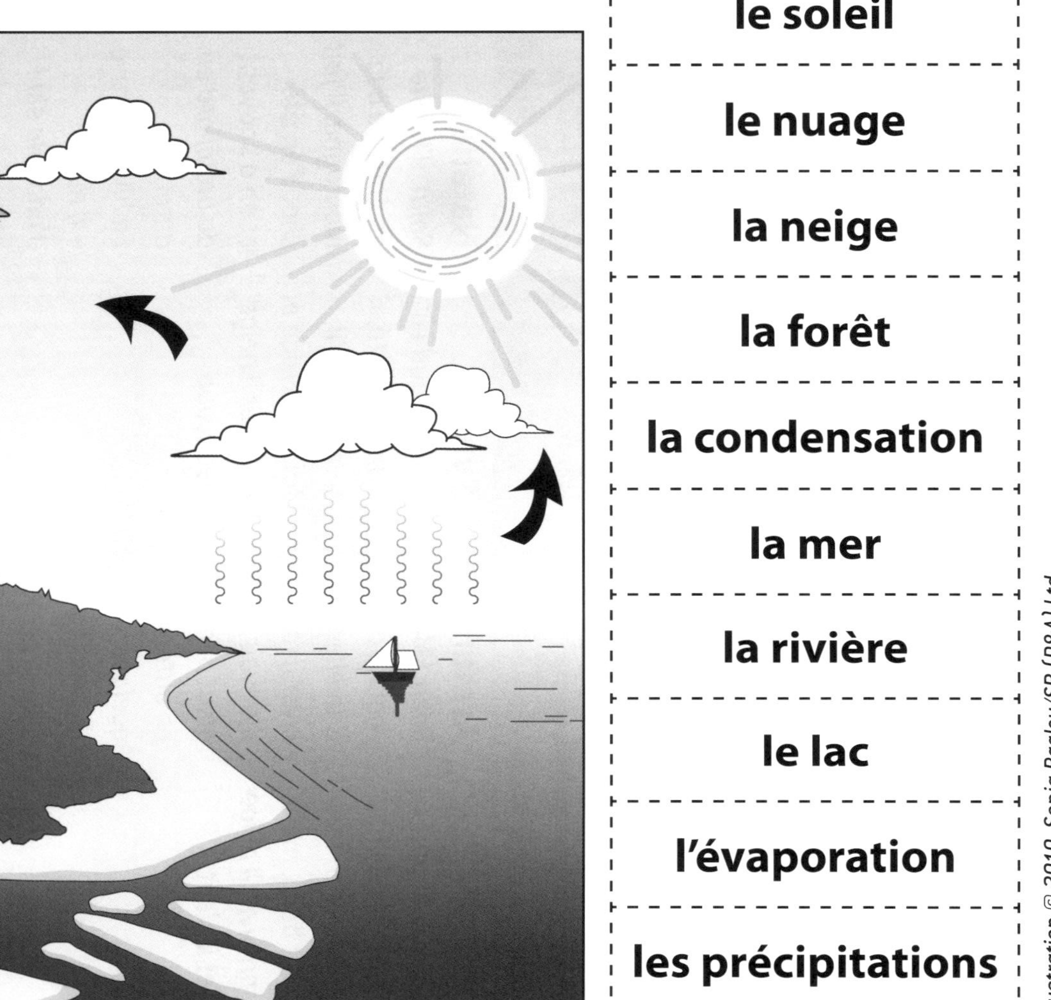

le soleil
le nuage
la neige
la forêt
la condensation
la mer
la rivière
le lac
l'évaporation
les précipitations

Quel temps fait-il en Europe ?

Anouk
J'habite dans l'ouest de la France. En été il fait beau, mais en hiver il neige et il pleut.

Armand
Salut ! Moi, j'habite à Bruxelles. En hiver il fait mauvais. Il pleut beaucoup en automne et quelquefois il fait du brouillard.

Sylvie
Il fait chaud en Suisse en été. Quelquefois il fait de l'orage et en hiver il neige beaucoup.

Natalie
Salut. J'habite en Andorre à la montagne. Il fait chaud en été et on a souvent du brouillard en automne. En hiver – bravo – il neige ! J'adore le ski !

Roman
Bonjour ! Il fait très chaud en Corse en été. Même au printemps il fait chaud et il fait du soleil.

1. Four of the children tell us about the weather in winter where they live. Draw weather symbols in each box below to show you understand what they say.

Anouk [ ] **Armand** [ ] **Sylvie** [ ] **Natalie** [ ]

2. Are the statements below *vrai ou faux* (true or false)?

A Bruxelles il neige en automne.	*Vrai/Faux*
Il fait chaud en Suisse en hiver.	*Vrai/Faux*
En Andorre il fait du brouillard en automne.	*Vrai/Faux*
En été en Corse il fait très chaud.	*Vrai/Fraux*

3. Can you finish these sentences?

En Suisse en été ______________________

En Andorre en hiver ______________________

Dans l'ouest de la France ______________________

____

Les dominos

LE DEPART	**Quel temps fait-il aujourd'hui?**
il fait chaud aussi.	**Quel temps fait-il**
fait froid aussi.	**Quel**
froid aussi.	**L'ARRIVEE**
fait-il aujourd'hui?	**Il fait très beau,**
temps fait-il	**aujourd'hui?**
Il y a du vent,	**il fait**
le soleil brille.	**Quel temps**
Il pleut,	**il neige et**
aujourd'hui?	**Il fait mauvais, il**

Prénom :

Ecris et dessine

Quand il neige, je porte un anorak et une écharpe.	*Quand il fait chaud, je porte* ____________ *et* ____________
Quand il pleut, je porte ____________	*Quand il fait du vent, je porte* ____________
Quand il fait froid, ____________	*Quand il fait du soleil,* ____________

je porte   un anorak   des baskets   une casquette   un chapeau

une écharpe   une jupe   un maillot de bain   un manteau   des mitaines

un pantalon   un pull   des sandales   un short   un T-shirt

Jeux

Unscramble the letters to find the weather phrases.

a d u h c i l f a i t _ _ _ _ _	 t l e u p i l _ _ _ _ _
 s o l i l e i l f a i t d u _ _ _ _ _ _	 n e v t i l f a i t d u _ _ _ _
 g n e i e i l _ _ _ _ _	 f e a u i i l _ a _ t b _ _ _
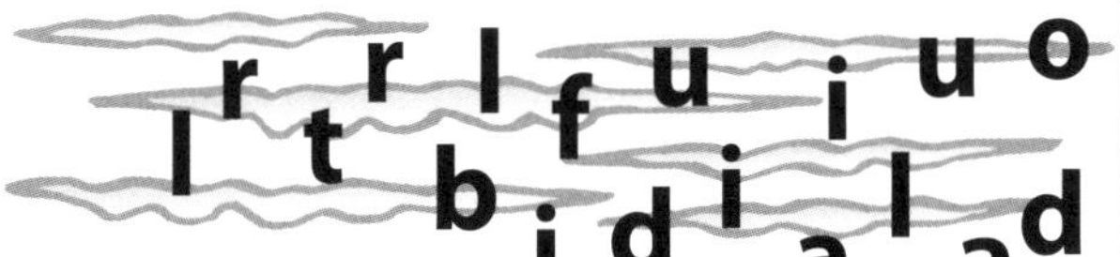 r r l f u i u o l t b i d i a l a d _	 f o e g a r a i a i _ l _ _ _ t d _ l' _ _ _ _ e

Find the months hidden in the snake.

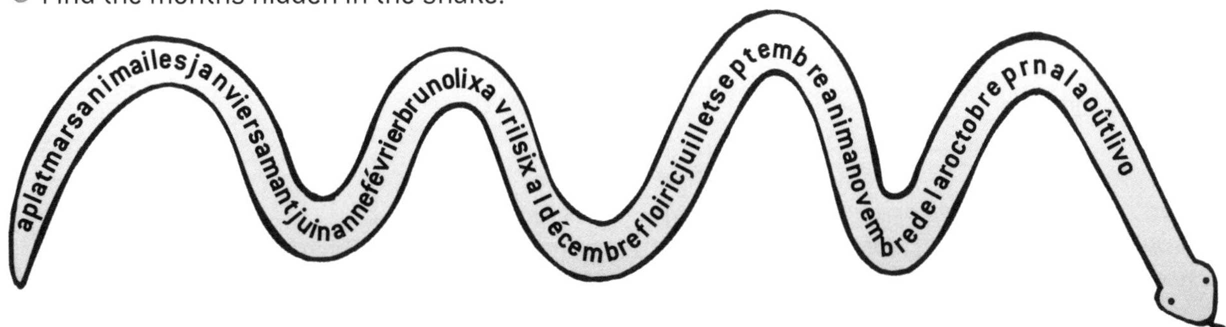

Glossary

General vocabulary

aujourd'hui .... today
aussi .... also/too
avec .... with
beaucoup (de).... lots (of)
bienvenue .... welcome
c'est .... it is
ce sont........... they are
chez moi .... at home
comme........... as/like
dans .... in
entre............. between
et................ and
génial............ great/smashing
je m'appelle ...... my name is
mais .... but
merci .... thank you
mon/ma/mes..... my
par an .... per year
parce que .... because
plus de........... more than
quand............ when
souvent .... often
super .... great/smashing
toujours.......... always/still
très.............. very
voilà .... there is/are

Topic-related vocabulary

Activities and sports

Quand il fait beau ...
.... When the weather is fine...
Quand il fait mauvais ...
.... When the weather is bad...
En vacances ... . On holiday...
j'aime .... I like...
je n'aime pas .... I don't like...
Tu aimes ... ? ..... Do you like...?
aller .... to go/going
aller à la piscine .. to go/going to the swimming pool
aller à la plage ... to go/going to the beach
aller au cinéma ... to go/going to the cinema
apprendre à cuisiner
.... to learn/learning to cook
danser........... to dance/dancing
faire de la poterie . (to do/doing) pottery
faire des châteaux de sable
.... to make/making sandcastles
faire des randonnées à cheval/à vélo
.... to go/going for horse/bike rides
faire du ski .... to ski/go skiing
faire du ski nautique
.... to waterski/go waterskiing
faire du snowboard
.... to snowboard/go snowboarding
faire du théâtre... (to do/doing) drama
faire du toboggan. to go/going tobogganing
faire du vélo ...... to cycle/cycling
faire une promenade
.... to go/going for a walk
jouer............. to play/playing
jouer au basket
.... to play/playing basketball
jouer au foot(ball) to play/playing football
jouer à l'ordinateur
.... play/playing on the computer
jouer au rugby.... to play/playing rugby
jouer au tennis ... to play/playing tennis
mes copains (m pl)
.... my friends
mon chien........ my dog
sauter à la corde.. to skip/skipping

Clothing

Qu'est-ce que je mets ... ?
.... What do I put on/am I putting on...?
je mets............. I put on...
pour me protéger . to protect me
je porte............. I'm wearing...
anorak (m)....... anorak
baskets (m pl).... trainers
bottes (f pl) ...... boots
bottes (f pl) *en caoutchouc*
.... wellington boots
casquette (f) ..... cap
chapeau (m) ..... hat
écharpe (f)....... scarf
jupe (f)........... skirt
lunettes (f pl) *de soleil*
.... sunglasses
maillot (m) *de bain*
.... swimsuit
manteau (m)..... coat
mitaines (f pl) .... mittens
pantalon (m)..... pair of trousers
parapluie (m) .... umbrella
pull (m).......... jumper
sac (m).......... bag
sandales (f pl).... sandals
short (m) .... pair of shorts
sweat (m)........ sweatshirt
T-shirt (m) .... T-shirt

Countries

j'habite........... I live
Andorre (f) .... Andorra
Belgique (f) ...... Belgium
Corse (f) .... Corsica
Espagne (f) ...... Spain
France (f) .... France
Sénégal (m)...... Senegal
Suisse (f) .... Switzerland
pays (m)......... country
le Midi............ France is sometimes referred to in this way due to its shape

Directions

nord (m) .... north
sud (m).......... south
est (m) .... east
ouest (m) .... west
nord-est (m) ..... north-east
nord-ouest (m)... north-west
sud-est (m) ...... south-east
sud-ouest (m).... south-west
centre (m) .... centre
hexagone (m) .... hexagon
Le vent souffle du nord/sud
.... The wind is blowing from the north/south
... est dans le sud/nord/centre
.... is in the south/north/centre
C'est dans le sud/nord/centre ?
.... Is it in the south/north/centre?
... de la France/la Belgique
.... of France/Belgium (feminine countries)
... de l'Angleterre.. of England
boussole (f)...... compass

Geographical features

capitale (f) .... capital
forêt (f).......... forest
île (f) .... island
lac (m)........... lake
Méditerranée (f) . Mediterranean
montagne (f)..... mountain
petit village (m) .. small village
Pyrénées (f) ..... Pyrenees
Pyrénées Atlantiques
.... Atlantic, used to refer to the Western Pyrenees
Pyrénées Occidentales
.... Eastern Pyrenees
rivière (f) .... river
toundra (f) .... tundra

très grande ville (f) .... very big town
très petite principauté (f) .... very small principality

Languages

je parle .... I speak
on parle .... We speak/one speaks
allemand (m) ..... German
anglais (m) .... English
catalan (m) ...... Catalan
flamand (m) ...... Flemish
français (m) ...... French
italien (m) .... Italian
romanche .... Romansh

Months

mois (m) .... month(s)
année (f) .... year
janvier .... January
février .... February
mars .... March
avril .... April
mai .... May
juin .... June
juillet .... July
août .... August
septembre .... September
octobre .... October
novembre .... November
décembre .... December
C'est quand, ton anniversaire ? .... When is your birthday?
Mon anniversaire, c'est en février .... My birthday is in February

Seasons

quatre saisons (f) four seasons
printemps (m) .... spring
été (m)........... summer
automne (m) ..... autumn
hiver (m) .... winter
C'est en quelle saison ? .... What season is it in?
au printemps ..... in spring
en été .... in summer
en automne ...... in autumn
en hiver .... in winter
ce sont .... these are...
mois (m pl) *de l'hiver* .... months of winter
mois d'été .... months of summer
mois d'automne .. months of autumn
mois de printemps months of spring
saison (f) *sèche* .. dry season
saison de (s) *pluie*(s) .... rainy season

The water cycle

brume (f)......... mist
chaleur (f)........ heat
chauffer .... to heat
colline (f)......... hill
condensation (f) .. condensation
eau (f) .... water
énergie solaire (f). sun's energy
gouttelette (f) .... droplet
mer (f) .... sea
océan (m)........ ocean
précipitation (f)... precipitation
rivière (f)......... river
terre (f) .... earth
transpiration (f) .. transpiration
évaporation (f) ... evaporation
le soleil brille ..... the sun shines
la neige fond...... the snow melts
l'eau s'évapore.... the water evaporates
la vapeur monte .. the water vapour rises
la vapeur devient froid .... the vapour gets cold
j'utilise l'eau pour ... . I use water for...
... laver les vêtements .... washing clothes
... boire ....drinking
... me laver les dents ....cleaning my teeth
... préparer les repas ....preparing meals
... faire la vaisselle ....doing the washing up

Trees

arbre (m)......... tree
écorce (f) .... bark
feuille (f) .... leaf
graine (f)......... seed

Weather

Quel temps fait-il ? .... What is the weather like?
Quel temps fait-il aujourd'hui ? .... What's the weather like today?
il fait beau .... the weather is fine
il fait chaud .... it's warm/hot
il fait de l'orage ... it's stormy
il fait du brouillard it's foggy
il fait du soleil..... it's sunny
il fait du vent ..... it's windy
il fait mauvais .... the weather is bad
il fait froid .... it's cold
il neige .... it's snowing
il pleut .... it's raining
il pleut à verse .... it's raining heavily
il y a du vent...... it's windy
il y a du brouillard. it's foggy
il y a du soleil ..... it's sunny
le soleil brille ..... the sun is shining

SCHOLASTIC

Also available in this series:

ISBN 978-1407-10203-0

ISBN 978-1407-10207-8

ISBN 978-1407-10208-5

ISBN 978-1407-10206-1

ISBN 978-1407-10205-4

ISBN 978-1407-10204-7